WASHINGTON, D.C. BY NIGHT

other cities in the **by Night** series

Amsterdam	Manhattan
Chicago	Miami
Las Vegas	New Orleans
London	Paris
Los Angeles	Prague
Madrid/Barcelona	San Francisco

Frommer's

WASHINGTON, D.C. by Night

BY

NICOLE ARTHUR

WITH CONTRIBUTIONS FROM

THEODORE FISCHER

A BALLIETT & FITZGERALD BOOK

MACMILLAN • USA

a disclaimer

Prices fluctuate in the course of time, and travel information changes under the impact of the varied and volatile factors that influence the travel industry. Neither the author nor the publisher can be held responsible for the experiences of readers while traveling. Readers are invited to write to the publisher with ideas, comments, and suggestions for future editions.

about the authors

Nicole Arthur is a Washington, D.C.-based writer.

Theodore Fischer is the author of *Cheap/Smart Travel, Cheap Smart Weekends, Frommer's Irreverent Guide to Washington, D.C.*, and literally billions of magazine travel stories.

Balliett & Fitzgerald, Inc.
Editorial director: Will Balliett
Executive editor: Tom Dyja
Production editor: Maria Fernandez
Associate editor: Sue Canavan
Editorial assistants: Rachel Florman, Margaret Hanscom, Aram Song, Ben Welch, and Paige Wilder

Macmillan Travel art director: Michele Laseau

MACMILLAN TRAVEL
A Simon & Schuster Macmillan Company
1633 Broadway
New York, NY 10019

ISBN 0-02-861879-3
Library of Congress information available from Library of Congress.

special sales

Bulk purchases (10+ copies) of Frommer's and selected Macmillan travel guides are available to corporations, organizations, institutions, and charities at special discounts, and can be customized to suit individual needs. For more information write to Special Sales, Macmillan General Reference, 1633 Broadway, New York, NY 10019.

Manufactured in the United States of America

contents

Washington, D.C., at a Glance

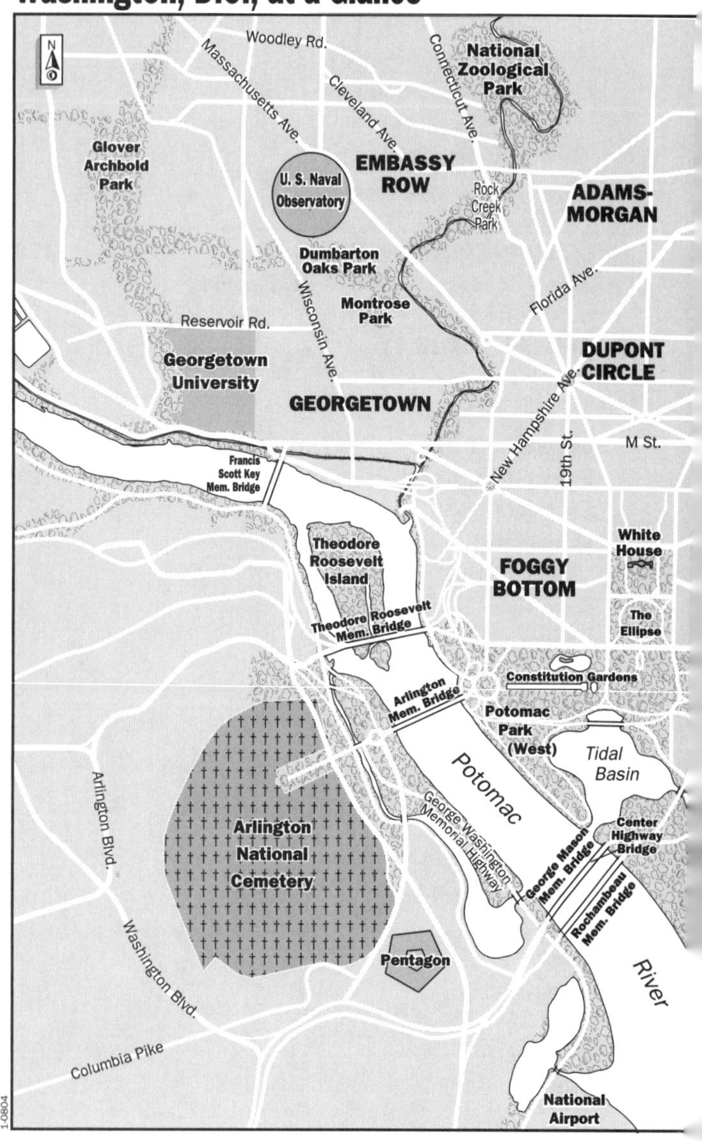

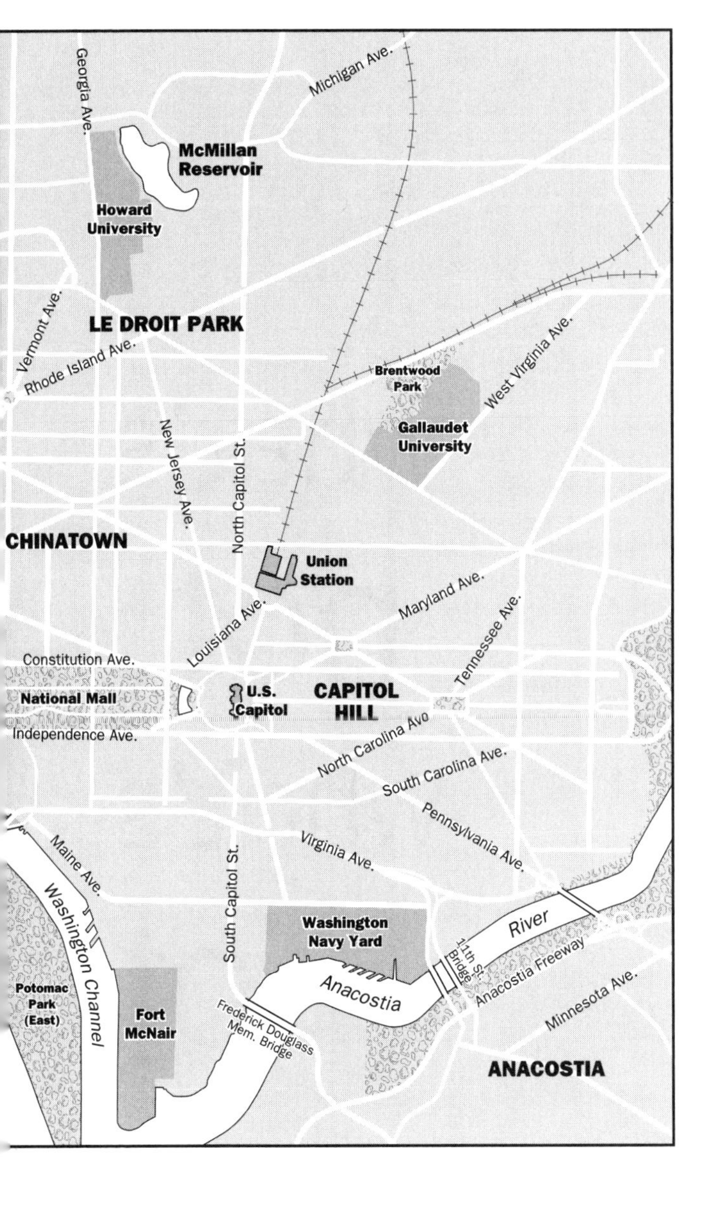

Georgia Ave.
Michigan Ave.
McMillan Reservoir
Howard University
Vermont Ave.
LE DROIT PARK
Rhode Island Ave.
Brentwood Park
West Virginia Ave.
Gallaudet University
New Jersey Ave.
North Capitol St.
CHINATOWN
Union Station
Maryland Ave.
Tennessee Ave.
Louisiana Ave.
Constitution Ave.
National Mall
U.S. Capitol
CAPITOL HILL
Independence Ave.
North Carolina Ave.
South Carolina Ave.
Pennsylvania Ave.
Virginia Ave.
Maine Ave.
Washington Channel
South Capitol St.
Washington Navy Yard
River
11th St. Bridge
Anacostia Freeway
Anacostia
Potomac Park (East)
Fort McNair
Frederick Douglass Mem. Bridge
Minnesota Ave.
ANACOSTIA

what's hot, what's not

On one hand it's a federal showplace, land o' fat-cat lobbyists and camera-toting tourists, with more marble and limestone per square mile than any city since imperial Rome. On the other hand, it's an urban debacle, a crime-infested ghetto city that actually reelected convicted drug user Marion Barry as its all-time favorite mayor. As a city, Washington, D.C. suffers one whale of an identity crisis.

Americans have been trying to make up their minds about it since the land it stands on was ceded by Maryland and Virginia in 1791; the site was a compromise between North and South and, like most compromises, doesn't please anyone. (To wit: John F. Kennedy's acerbic observation that the city exudes "Southern efficiency and Northern charm.") Through the early 19th century, foreign diplomats posted in Washington received hardship allowances. Many of the city's contemporary residents think *they* should, too. This is a metropolis with many residents and few natives—the only spot in America that doesn't have its own voting congressmen—so everyone feels free to whine about its shortcomings. Whether that whining is always justified is another question.

Nowhere are the misperceptions more persistent than in the realm of D.C.'s nightlife. First Lady Abigail Adams once famously described the nation's capital as "a sleepy Southern town," and that's an image that has stuck fast. Washington hasn't moved since then (although its most southerly acreage was retroceded to Virginia in 1846), but an influx of high-energy inhabitants from the North and every foreign country under the sun makes the city today distinctly un-Southern and anything but sleepy after the sun goes down. In today's Washington, plain-vanilla bureaucrats by day morph into party creatures of the night. Wide awake into the wee hours, they restlessly support a nightlife scene characterized by ample quantity, real variety, uneven quality, and—more than in any other American city we can think of—congenial mingling of the races.

Yes, there are legions of policy wonks who head straight from their government offices to their tidy suburban homes at night; these high-profile Washingtonians have little or nothing to do with D.C. nightlife. All the better for D.C. nightlife, say the real revelers. You'll generally find four local demographic cohorts out at night: students from the many area colleges plus high-schoolers with wheels; young, single, urban professionals—the friends of *Friends*—grabbing some gusto before family responsibilities end nightlife as they know it; foreigners reared in societies where the cultural norm involves going out often and staying out late; and a large and active gay and lesbian population. Locals are joined in their frolics by frisky tourists and expense-account-wielding businesspeople.

The nighttime pleasures of greater Washington (which encompasses broad swathes of northern Virginia and southern Maryland within and beyond the Beltway) range all over the spectrum, from the bowl of plastic wind-up toys tucked under the bar at Atomic Billiards in Cleveland Park, to the propulsive thump of D.C.'s native go-go at the Capitol City Pavilion in Northwest, to the conveyor belt of doughnuts moving toward the thick cascade of glaze at the Krispy Kreme in Alexandria. And then there's always that heady Capraesque feeling you get as you approach the capital's monument-punctuated skyline by night—it can send a shiver up the most jaded spine.

What's hot

U Street... "The New U," a three-block stretch of U Street, NW, is home to the city's highest concentration of hip clubs, stores, and restaurants. There's **Millennium,** a retro mini-mall that's the place to go for chrome cocktail shakers and Formica-topped tables, the sleek **Republic Gardens** nightclub (which takes its name from a jazz venue that occupied the site in the forties), Soviet-themed acid-jazz hangout **State of the Union,** and many others. Once known as "The Black Broadway" and home to many of the city's legendary performers—not least native son Duke Ellington—the area was among those hardest hit by the 1968 riots. These days, thanks in part to a newly opened Metro stop (U Street-Cardozo), the renovation of the historic **Lincoln Theater,** and the close proximity of rock clubs like the **9:30** and the **Black Cat,** U Street is literally booming.

Cigars... The backlash had to come sometime. Perhaps it was one too many "Thank You for Not Smoking" signs, but something brought on Washington's defiant cigar craze. Downtown's **Ozio,** which bills itself as "a martini and cigar lounge," has a glass-walled humidor as its centerpiece. Meanwhile, every place from the stodgy **Basin Street Lounge** to trendy **Felix** has instigated cigar- and/or martini-themed nights. You can buy cigars to puff while you play pool at **The Rock,** and chef Roberto Donna's upscale Italian restaurant **Galileo** has outdone everyone by installing the city's first cigar vending machine.

Rat Pack cool... Echoes from a more sophisticated era have tempered the city's uncouth nightlife. Where once there was Pabst Blue Ribbon there are now martinis. There's a proliferation of nightspots with the word "lounge" in the name, as if the word alone were enough to confer coolness. (It isn't, but it comes close.) Twentysomethings have rediscovered classic jazz and its postmodern counterpart, acid jazz. Even the **Black Cat,** a scruffy alternative rock club, hosts the Black Cat Ball, an actual swing dance featuring an actual big band. So what if it's attended by a crowd of young hipsters raised in mosh pits, who have no idea how to dance with a partner?

Artful happy hours... Several Washington museums invite you into their galleries after hours to schmooze and cruise with microbrews (plus chardonnay and munchies). While chitchat tends to be more political than artistic, the art museum setting provides an elevated and civilized alternative to the bar scene. The **Corcoran Museum of Art** and **Phillips Collection** started the trend, but now other museums and a number of the private galleries also know what you like. Check listings in the Washington *Post* and *City Paper* to find out where it's at, or see the Hanging Out chapter.

The eighties... Though the nineties are drawing to a close, you're as likely to spend an evening out in D.C. listening to Human League and New Order as you are, say, Nine Inch Nails. Ahead of the curve, **Club Heaven** has the city's longest-running eighties night, while new clubs like **Decades** and **Polly Esther's** are hedging their bets with both seventies and eighties music. If the number of local clubs that now feature retro music nights is any indication, a lot of people out there are baffled by contemporary dance music. (House? Trance? Jungle? Do you have any Duran Duran?) As for the ascendancy of the eighties, perhaps the explanation lies in the overexposure of seventies hip (see What's Not).

What's not

Georgetown... It's tempting (and reasonably accurate) to dismiss Georgetown with the old Yogi Berra line: "Nobody goes there any more; it's too crowded." Gridlocked traffic (unrelieved by Metro service), cutthroat competition for scarce parking spaces, and lengthy lines for the popular haunts are caused mostly by bridge-and-beyond-the-Beltway people, not to mention outright out-of-towners. Those who know better long ago decamped for Adams-Morgan and the "New U," and they have an eye on the Penn Quarter/MCI Arena area (roughly between Pennsylvania Avenue and H Street, NW, from 6th to 9th streets), likely site of tomorrow's what's-hot nightlife district.

Coffee... Maybe it's just wishful thinking, but the whole coffee craze is beginning to lose its novelty. (Not that there isn't a Starbucks on every corner, and a Starbucks next door to the Starbucks—there's even one in Chinatown with a sign in Cantonese.) This we ascribe to the declining popularity of grunge and, by association, all things Seattle. Times have changed: Not even Courtney Love is grunge anymore. Another sign of coffee's waning status is the slow but steady encroachment of tea. Dupont Circle's **Teaism,** whose menu includes tea milk shakes, is the most crowded caffeine joint in town, while many of the chain coffee bars now have prominent tea displays. **Brothers,** for instance, offers a tasty orange-spice tea. Besides, you can buy Water Joe (super-caffeinated bottled water) at any **Sutton Place Gourmet**. Makes a skim latte look positively indulgent.

Microbrews... Downtown's **Capitol City Brewing Company** has long been a happy-hour mainstay, and similar microbars have recently opened in outlying areas: the **Virginia Beverage Company** in Alexandria and **Rock Bottom** in Bethesda. But this proliferation of designer breweries is a sure sign they're out as far as hipsters are concerned; once your scene is co-opted by the suburbs, you're in trouble. The fact is that mixed drinks are hot (see "Cigars" and "Rat Pack cool" in What's Hot), at least with the in crowd.

The Electric Slide... The Electric Slide came earlier and stayed later in D.C. The city can't often claim to be cutting edge, but this particular dance, that staple of wedding receptions, was invented by local DJ "Moon Man" Bacote. A longtime jock on WOL-AM, Bacote also spun records at local supper clubs, where he improvised the dance, a variation on that fifties shuffle, the bus stop. To everything there is a season.

Karaoke... If your idea of a good time is downing one Coors Light too many and singing "Close to You" to a roomful of strangers, you may be out of luck. Karaoke never really caught on in D.C., perhaps because it's a town in which so much effort is expended trying *not* to look stupid in public. This should not, however, be taken as an indication that the city is immune to silliness—to its credit, it recently weathered a drag bingo craze.

The seventies... Haven't we suffered the seventies revival long enough? The clothes at Georgetown's **Urban Outfitters**—where you can spend a fortune buying an ensemble identical to the one you wore in your third-grade class picture—are enough to stop seventies nostalgia in its tracks. You can still hear classic disco all over town but, tellingly, no club caters exclusively to seventies tastes. Another sign of the times: D.C.'s seventies radio station, WGAY, 99.5 FM, where you could count on hearing "How Deep Is Your Love" every hour on the hour, recently went under. It now plays "relaxing favorites," including a program of show tunes on Sunday morning. Who can say what this bodes, trendwise? Time marches inexorably forward; the eighties stand next in line for a comeback (see What's Hot). Whether or not that's an improvement is anyone's call.

the clu

1

b scene

At first glance, the image you get from C-SPAN doesn't seem all that far off: Washington is a daytime town, full of bureaucrats who work in, and on the periphery of, the federal government and flee to the suburbs at night. The club scene here is much less prominent than its counterparts in New York or L.A., where nightlife is touted as a natural resource. But if you know where to look, you'll find that D.C.'s smaller but no less spirited after-dark scene has much to recommend it. For one thing, you rarely have to stand in line, or be looked over (and overlooked) by some snooty bouncer at the door. For another thing, D.C.'s rich local music tradition fills the clubs with enthusiastic live bands and their devoted fans. Finally, it's in the clubs that Washington proves it does have an egalitarian soul. Though the town continues to be largely segregated in its neighborhoods, racially mixed and gay/straight crowds are becoming more the norm. Thanks to crossover music such as house and acid jazz, a broad band of colors and cultures come together at night. Once the high-profile dark suits are gone, those Washingtonians who actually like to have fun can finally come into their own.

The characteristic Washington yearning to be all things to all people is reflected in its clubs—often within the same club. The trend is toward one club doing different things on different nights, or even hosting different activities on the same night but in various parts of the building. It's increasingly difficult to designate some place a "jazz club" or a "punk club," or to label a venue a "restaurant" or "club": Many restaurants turn into dance clubs on weekends and during the week after the dinner crowd clears out.

In this eclectic, if somewhat small-volume, club scene, you can still find traditional funk and punk but, thanks to the city's diverse population and large international crowd, you can also can dip into a multiracial cocktail of music and dance. Just remember: In Washington, it's not where you go, it's who you're with. And on the latter count, you're on your own.

The Music Beat

What Washington does best as a club town is show off its indigenous live music—music that somehow defines the quality and character of the city itself. Two musical movements were born here, and they are as different as, well, black and white: go-go and harDCore.

As the influence of punk rock made itself felt in the

U.S., distinctive punk subgenres began to appear in many big American cities. In D.C., Ian MacKaye's Minor Threat set the moralistic tone of what came to be known as harDCore by rejecting commercial success and embracing an ascetic creed called "straight edge." (The term came from a 1982 Minor Threat song—"I've got better things to do...laugh at the thought of eating 'Ludes/Laugh at the thought of sniffing glue...I've got the straight edge.") Several big names are footnotes to the D.C. scene: Henry Rollins was in the Teen Idles before decamping for California, while Nirvana drummer Dave Grohl spent time in Scream and currently owns a share in D.C.'s Black Cat nightclub. But perhaps the most significant legacy of the era—not counting the harDCore reverberations in the sound of bands like Green Day—is Dischord Records, the still flourishing independent record label co-founded by MacKaye and Minor Threat drummer Jeff Nelson. Today, MacKaye fronts Fugazi, one of the best-selling independent acts ever—and still charges only $5 per show.

Washington also has a homegrown style of funk known as go-go. Wildly popular in D.C.'s African-American community, go-go evolved during the mid-seventies when local R&B artist Chuck Brown began to liven up the cover songs he played by adding complex layers of percussion. Brown had a national hit in 1978 with "Busting Loose," and since then go-go has occasionally made its way to the national charts. Its biggest 15 seconds in the national spotlight came in 1988 when Experience Unlimited performed "Da Butt" in Spike Lee's movie *School Daze.*

Though go-go is mostly a regional music, dozens of bands have thrived here over the past 20 years: Go-go lineups can fill the area's sports arenas. There are now several generations playing varying go-go styles. There's the old-school classic sound of Brown, Trouble Funk, Rare Essence, and Experience Unlimited, as well as the harder, hip-hop influenced new generation (local faves include the Northeast Groovers, Pure Elegance, the Huckabucks, the Backyard Band, and the Junkyard Band). The best way to find out about go-go shows is to look for the fluorescent Globe posters along Georgia Avenue, NW. WPGC-FM features a go-go half-hour at 9:30pm weeknights, and has a go-go hot line.

Of course, not all the chapters in D.C.'s musical history are the kind you want to re-read. Case in point: the Starland Vocal Band's "Afternoon Delight," which consistently makes the Top 10 in Dave Barry's "Worst Songs of All Time" poll.

The band scored this number-one hit—its only top-40 record—in the bad-taste banner year of 1976. Local songwriter Bill Danoff, incidentally, got the idea from the name of a lunch special at Clyde's restaurant in Georgetown (see Late Night Dining).

At the city's "concert clubs," dancing and drinking are incidental. These are places where you come to see the show rather than hang out, if only because ticket prices can be pretty steep. (Both 9:30 Club and the Black Cat have separate bars, but neither is a stand-alone attraction.) National acts often sell out, and tickets are available in advance from club box offices or by phone through TicketMaster (tel 202/432–SEAT) or Protix (tel 703/218–6500). The 9:30 uses Protix; the Black Cat, Capitol Ballroom, Bayou, and Birchmere use TicketMaster.

Getting Past the Velvet Rope

At dance clubs proper, there are blessedly few lines in D.C., and little New York–style club 'tude. Image-conscious downtown dance clubs like **Club Zei** and the **Spy Club** have lines, but they're mostly for show; they seldom actually turn anyone away. The only D.C. club that has an exclusionary door policy is the **Eighteenth Street Lounge,** and then only on weekends. As for what it takes to get in there, it helps to be good-looking and dress cool—doesn't it always?—but plenty of hepcats and kittens are sent packing, too.

Adams-Morgan and Dupont Circle Clubs

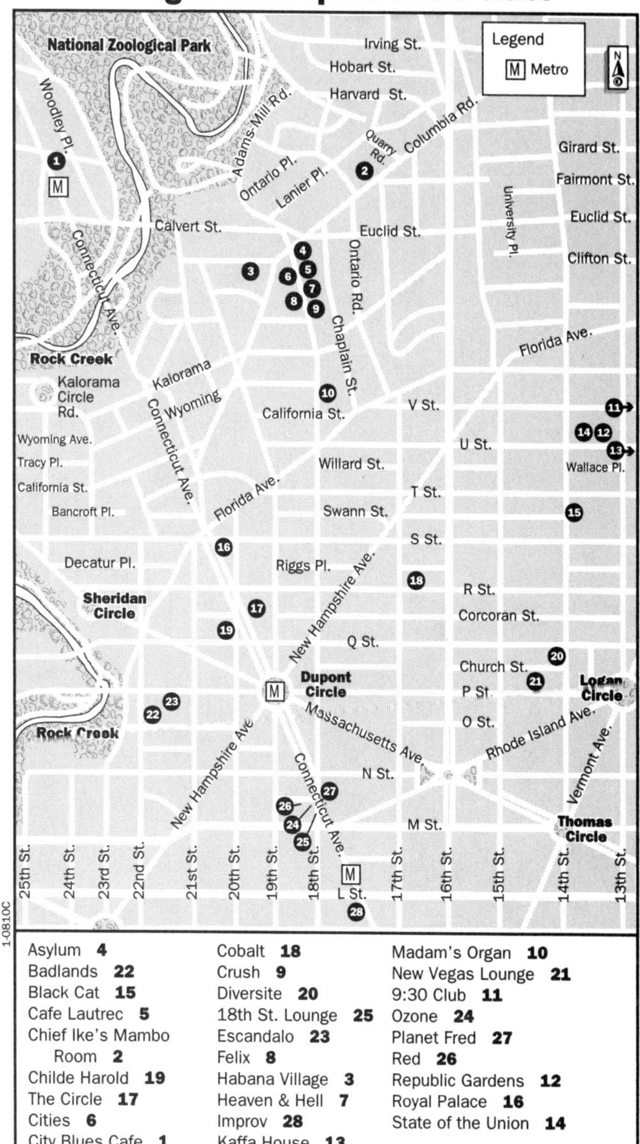

Asylum **4**
Badlands **22**
Black Cat **15**
Cafe Lautrec **5**
Chief Ike's Mambo Room **2**
Childe Harold **19**
The Circle **17**
Cities **6**
City Blues Cafe **1**
Cobalt **18**
Crush **9**
Diversite **20**
18th St. Lounge **25**
Escandalo **23**
Felix **8**
Habana Village **3**
Heaven & Hell **7**
Improv **28**
Kaffa House **13**
Madam's Organ **10**
New Vegas Lounge **21**
9:30 Club **11**
Ozone **24**
Planet Fred **27**
Red **26**
Republic Gardens **12**
Royal Palace **16**
State of the Union **14**

Georgetown & Downtown Clubs

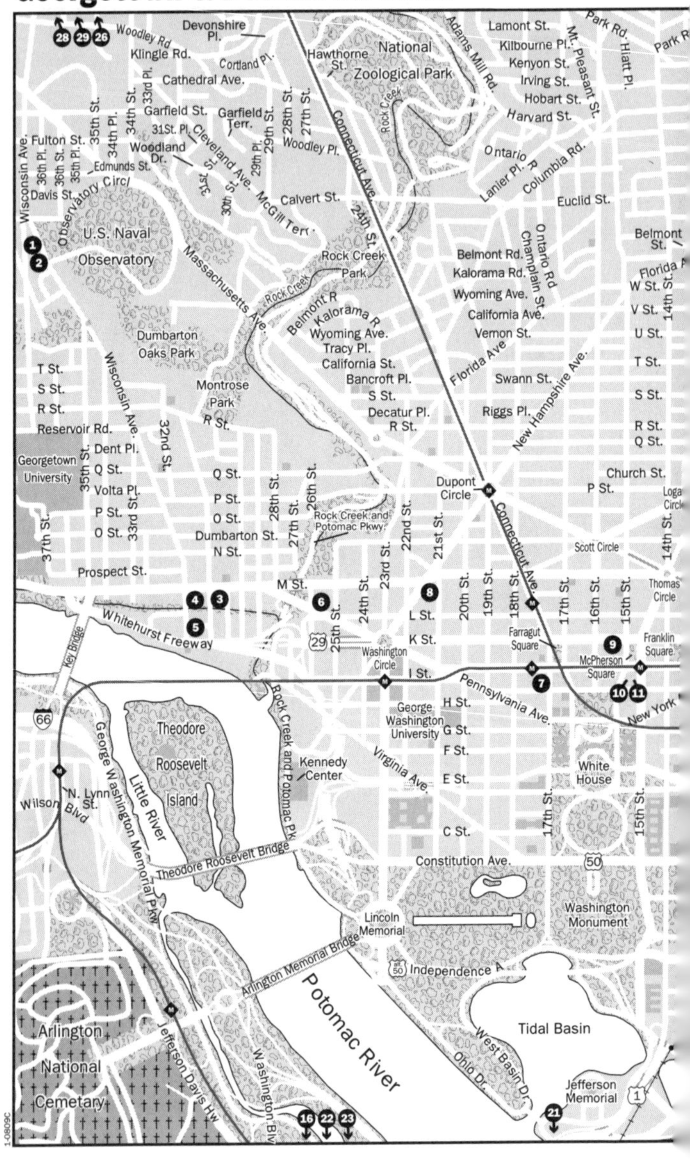

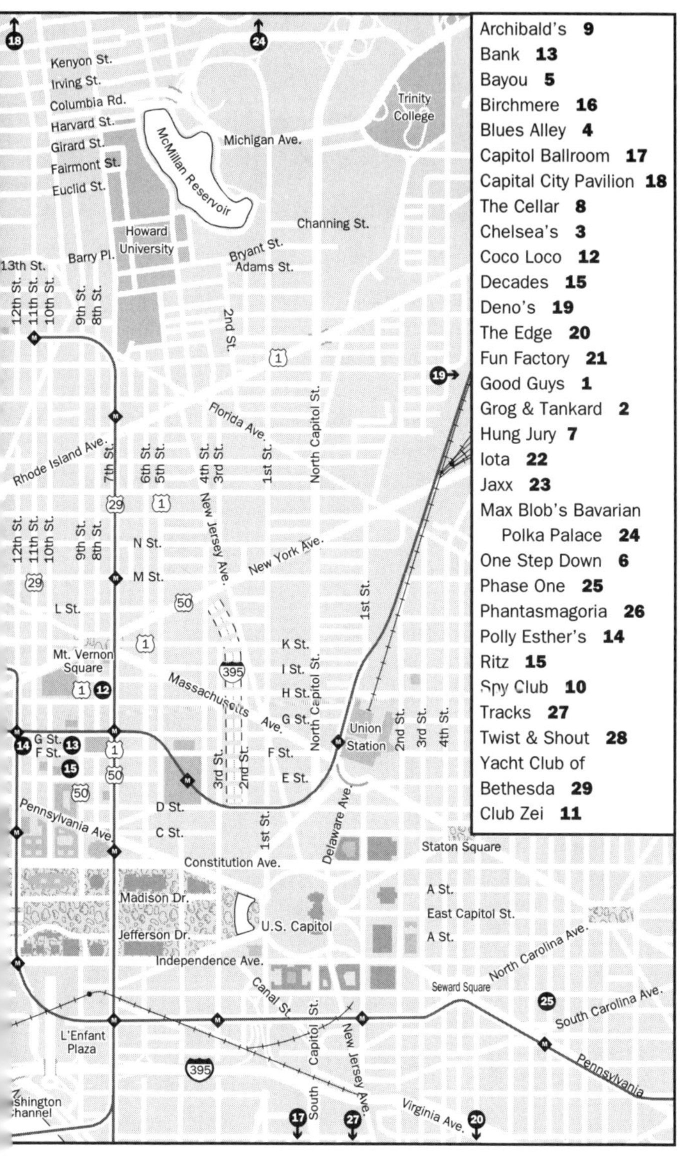
Archibald's 9
Bank 13
Bayou 5
Birchmere 16
Blues Alley 4
Capitol Ballroom 17
Capital City Pavilion 18
The Cellar 8
Chelsea's 3
Coco Loco 12
Decades 15
Deno's 19
The Edge 20
Fun Factory 21
Good Guys 1
Grog & Tankard 2
Hung Jury 7
Iota 22
Jaxx 23
Max Blob's Bavarian Polka Palace 24
One Step Down 6
Phase One 25
Phantasmagoria 26
Polly Esther's 14
Ritz 15
Spy Club 10
Tracks 27
Twist & Shout 28
Yacht Club of Bethesda 29
Club Zei 11
Kenyon St.
Irving St.
Columbia Rd.
Harvard St.
Girard St.
Fairmont St.
Euclid St.
McMillan Reservoir
Michigan Ave.
Trinity College
Channing St.
Howard University
Barry Pl.
Bryant St.
Adams St.
13th St.
12th St.
11th St.
10th St.
9th St.
8th St.
2nd St.
Florida Ave.
North Capitol St.
Rhode Island Ave.
7th St.
6th St.
5th St.
4th St.
3rd St.
1st St.
New Jersey Ave.
N St.
M St.
New York Ave.
L St.
Mt. Vernon Square
K St.
I St.
H St.
G St.
F St.
E St.
Massachusetts Ave.
Union Station
D St.
C St.
Pennsylvania Ave.
Delaware Ave.
Staton Square
Constitution Ave.
Madison Dr.
Jefferson Dr.
U.S. Capitol
A St.
East Capitol St.
Independence Ave.
Canal St.
North Carolina Ave.
Seward Square
South Carolina Ave.
L'Enfant Plaza
South Capitol St.
Virginia Ave.
Pennsylvania

The Lowdown

The politics of dancing... The fact is that after-hours D.C. is refreshingly nonpartisan—party affiliation never bailed anybody out on the dance floor. There's something for both sides of the aisle at U Street's **State of the Union:** Lefties can pay homage to the massive rendering of Lenin, while right-wingers can gaze on the commie iconography and dream that the Cold War never ended. Both parties can dance to the club's funky acid jazz. If the near-body-cavity search upon entering **Tracks** weren't enough to give the Christian Coalition the heebie-jeebies, the out-and-proud ethos of this huge, gay-owned dance club will, not to mention the fact that a fair number of straight-looking straights are on the dance floor consorting with the gays. Meanwhile, the writhing, spandex-clad crowd of beautiful young internationals at **Club Zei** gives new meaning to the phrase "body politic."

Clinton family values... When young D.C. talks about Clinton, it means Chelsea. The First Daughter—dubbed "DOTUS," an acronym for "daughter of the United States" by the *Post*'s gossip column—is no stranger to D.C. clubs. She was recently spotted rocking out to "All I Wanna Do" at Sheryl Crow's sold-out **9:30 Club** gig. Somebody had to drag the family's musical taste kicking and screaming into the nineties—keep in mind that Bill Clinton's idea of establishing street credibility was adopting Fleetwood Mac's "Don't Stop" as an unofficial campaign song. (Unfortunately, the tie-in wasn't enough to reverse the fortunes of Fleetwood's, the now-defunct Alexandria blues club co-owned by the band's drummer, Mick Fleetwood. That must explain the band's 1997 reunion tour.)

Rock steady... Seeing as how it's smack dab in the middle of the East Coast, Washington is a stop on just about every major and not-so-major rock tour going. The city has a variety of reasonably sized rock clubs, namely venues that aren't so mammoth that they accommodate major sporting events on off nights. The most venerable of these is the **9:30 Club,** until recently located in downtown D.C. The old club was home to a legendarily inexplicable smell, which *Washington City Paper,* the local alternative weekly, hired an expert to decode. His verdict: beer-soaked wood. These days, the far less cramped and far less smelly 9:30 is in a newly renovated space with upstairs and downstairs bars (ask for "the blue thing," its signature frozen cocktail.) The new space was formerly the WUST Radio Music Hall, the broadcast performance space for a gospel radio station; in its decline, the hall was rented out as a rock and hip-hop venue. The 9:30's renovation, among other things, entailed painting over the peeling John Henry mural that once graced one end of the building. The central floor is about the size of a basketball court, encircled by a balcony of tiered seating. It's still in a lousy neighborhood, but, hey, it's a *different* lousy neighborhood. The crowd varies with the shows; a recent Friday night saw back-to-back performances by folkie Suzanne Vega and a metal outfit called the Genitorturers. The scene on the sidewalk as one audience left and the other arrived was worth the price of admission.

The 9:30 Club finally has a little competition from the **Black Cat,** a relatively new arrival that books indie bands like Sleater-Kinney and Sebadoh. The Cat styles itself as a younger, hipper 9:30, which, to a large extent, it is. Because it books fewer mainstream acts, it draws fewer suburbanites and more slumping guys wearing vintage bowling shirts with "Earl" stitched over the pocket (a sure sign that they were program directors at their college radio stations). Unlike the 9:30, it's a hangout—the kind of place you would consider going even if there was a bad band or no band. Pool tables and dilapidated tables and chairs lend a bar-room ambiance to on stage proceedings. Across town, the **Capitol Ballroom** is a rock venue that books both alternative acts like the Foo Fighters and Bjork and DJs like the Chemical Brothers; it doubles as a 120-beats-per-minute dance club. The space, which looks a little too much like the set of Janet Jackson's "Rhythm

Nation" video, is the site of an insanely popular industrial night—which is altogether appropriate, since the club is located in an immense old boiler factory.

Hippest scenes... The ultrasuave **Eighteenth Street Lounge** is a sort of cocktail-nation/acid-jazz hybrid that attracts a mix of see-and-be-seen-sters, techno-heads, neo-beatniks, and whoever is buying all those Tony Bennett concert tickets. The multilevel club is strewn with squishy old couches, illuminated mostly by candlelight, and decorated with classic jazz record sleeves. DJs play everything from cool jazz to jungle to bossa nova to trip-hop, depending on the night of the week. ESL even has its own record label and its own glossy newsletter, in which club DJs include top-20 playlists consisting entirely of music that you've never heard of. If you have doubts about your own hipness quotient, you'd best go on a weeknight, when the club isn't crowded and its intermittent members-only policy is not an issue.

Outlandishly themed destinations are less a part of the D.C. nightlife landscape than they were five years ago, in the heyday of the Andalusian Dog (a Dali-themed restaurant whose facade was draped with melting clocks), and the Insect Club (whose bar snacks included crunchy dried crickets). But among the theme clubs that still thrive, foremost is the funky U Street nightspot **State of the Union,** which plays off the city's fascination with political figures with pre-glasnost hammer-and-sickle decor, 36 different vodkas, and a scowling bust of Lenin on the facade outside. At State, fin de siècle decrepitude meets live reggae. When hypnotic acid jazz is spinning on a crowded weekend night, the line of patrons—the pierced, the dreadlocked, and everybody else in their 20s and looking to dance—snakes out the door.

A cover, a dress code, and an attitude... Among the U Street Corridor's new, trendy clubs, none is trendier than **Republic Gardens,** a haven for Armani-upscale professional urbanites. The interior design by local sculptor Robert Cole—steel sheeting adorns the tables, mirrors, light fixtures, and bars—gives this town-house club considerable panache. (The life-size steel sculptures don't hurt, either.) DJs and occasional live music drown out conversation on the crowded upstairs dance floor. Don't even think about wearing a baseball cap. At the **Ritz,**

directly across the street from the Federal Bureau of Investigation, there are five "subclubs" on four floors: live jazz downstairs, reggae, hip-hop, and house elsewhere. The decor in this erstwhile commercial space includes Matisse-inspired murals on cobalt-blue walls and what appears to be a taxidermied wedding dress in the stairwell. The crowd is a mix of preening city dwellers and suburbanites up for a big night out. This is not the place for slumming; the club's dress code insists on jackets for men.

Terrifying **Club Zei,** housed in an old Pepco substation, is more like a Hollywood set designer's concept of an urban nightclub than an actual urban nightclub. It has a towering wall of video screens at one end, raised pedestals for exhibitionist solo dancing, and a massive lighting grid that swoops up and down. This club's affected exclusivity—its Zei-tgeist, if you will—means the cover's too high and that you stand in line with lacquered Eurotrash even when there's not a crowd inside. Oh, and you can't wear tennis shoes. A short walk down Zei Alley in tottering high heels, the **Spy Club** has similar pretensions and an equally long line that looks and sounds like Club Zei's, with even less English spoken. The interior, however, trades in Zei's post-industrial decor for gilt-edged paintings and candlelight. Both clubs play the requisite house/techno mix.

You make me feel like dancing... **Tracks** is *the* Washington dance club. This sprawling warehouse space in Southeast is gay-owned and operated—"If you have difficulty functioning in a gay environment, please do not enter," reads a large notice at the door—but its clientele is a demographic free-for-all. Everybody from raving queens to ravers takes over the place at some point during the week (call ahead to pin down the ever-changing schedule, or check things out online at http://www.tracks2000.com.). Tracks' main dance floor is reputed to be the largest on the East Coast, which is easy to believe; it can be surveyed comfortably from bleachers at one side.

Downtown, **Ozone** is the place to hear the latest in molar-vibrating house, techno, and jungle. The cult of the DJ is alive and well at this glass-fronted, multistoried, strobe-lit dance space; attendance at its Thursday night "Where the Wild Things Are" dance party is mandatory for precocious young scenesters. Around the corner, **Red,** a "subterranean discotheque" in a no-frills basement space, throbs with migraine-caliber techno until the wee hours. The crowd here is young enough to think dancing till 4am sounds like fun, and just old enough not to be grounded for blowing their curfew. Across Connecticut Avenue is **Planet Fred,** a sci-fi themed dance club whose walls are molded to look like lunar surfaces. The music here is a house/techno/top-40 mix, the dancers similarly eclectic; just don't make the mistake I recently did and accidentally go on "under 21" night (unless, of course, you are). Planet Fred hosts the Washington Psychotronic Film Society on Tuesdays for showings of the finest B movies ever made.

The Bank is the latest nightclub to take over the bank building on F Street, NW, across from the old 9:30 Club. Inside, under the domed, vaulted ceiling, dry ice vapors periodically roll onto the dance floor to the strains of house, techno, dancehall, and reggae. If you're an architecture buff—this is surely the city's most physically impressive dance space—or just like the idea of dancing alone on a pedestal under a spotlight, this is the place for you. Ads for **The Cellar,** an immense underground dance space italicized in green neon, claim that its DJs play "music that everybody knows." They should have added, "and wishes they didn't." This is where you'll find the college-age big-hair crowd. **Capitol Ballroom** hosts a massive Friday-night dance party called "Buzz" that features cutting-edge DJs and dance music's very latest permutations. For information about the city's weekly dance parties, go to Music Now in Georgetown and 12" Records in Dupont Circle and check out all the fliers.

All that jazz... Like much else in Washington, jazz clubs tread an egalitarian road, featuring an eclectic range of everything from fusion to old-style trios. The town's premiere jazz club is, confusingly enough, Georgetown's **Blues Alley,** which has the ambience of an upscale supper club, perhaps because it *is* an upscale supper club (pre-show dinner is available, though not obligatory). The low-ceilinged, brick-walled space is small enough to afford patrons an up-close look at their idols—indeed, you're liable to find some guy's saxophone in your soup. Recent acts have included everyone from Wynton Marsalis to Keith Jarrett. For those who find Blues Alley overpriced or snooty—two common complaints—there's nearby **One Step Down** on Pennsylvania Avenue, which books a higher percentage of local jazzers. With booths lining one side of the club and an ever-popular jazz jukebox playing, One Step Down sometimes resembles an extremely hip diner. In Adams-Morgan, neighborhood bar and restaurant **Cafe Lautrec** has nightly live jazz. It's easy to spot this crowded bistro-style hangout: Just look for the stories-high Toulouse-Lautrec-style mural on the front of the building.

Bluer than blue... Tucked into the middle of an uninhabited-looking block of P Street, NW, the **New Vegas Lounge** is as authentically shabby a blues joint as you could imagine. The club, with its tiny tables, weak red lighting, and flickering beer signs, is presided over by owner and occasional performer Dr. Blues. A favorite hangout of all sorts of touring musicians who pass through D.C.—Stephen Stills is one vocal admirer—the New Vegas is the only dive in town with a dress code. Now *that's* style. At the other extreme is the **City Blues Cafe,** a yuppie restaurant and live blues venue that is the button-down alternative to New Vegas. Note for the unadventurous: It's in Woodley Park's restaurant row and therefore doesn't necessitate a trip to a crummy neighborhood. **Madam's Organ,** Adams-Morgan's ramshackle neo-bohemian dive, has bright red walls and near nightly blues. For current information about blues performances in the city, call the D.C. Blues Society at 202/828–3028.

Gay and lesbian clubs... Washington's abundant gay nightlife is concentrated in two areas: Dupont Circle (hence its 1970s nickname, "the Fruit Loop") and southeast D.C. Tip for the lazy: In the single block of P Street, NW, between 21st and 22nd streets, there are five different gay bars and dance clubs. (And no parking places—take the Metro if possible.) Unprepossessing from the outside, the hulking peach-colored edifice called **Badlands** houses two bars and a spacious dance floor. A young male crowd comes out in full force to dance; most nights a line is guaranteed. Elsewhere in the circle, a young Latin crowd dances at **Escándalo!** and fashionable guppies congregate at **Cobalt**. The latter is designated only by a glowing blue square over the doorway—and the pulse of its mightily loud music. **The Fraternity House,** in the alley between P and O streets, has exactly the atmosphere you would expect at a place that has the rep for being Dupont Circle's top cruise bar. Expect to be thoroughly looked over. At the opposite end of the sleaze spectrum is **The Circle,** a stylish, tri-level, glass-fronted club that attracts an older, racially mixed crowd, both straight and gay. The upper-level terrace is Dupont Circle's most hotly contested outdoor space in summer.

Tracks, where drag queens and college kids often share the enormous dance floor, reigns supreme over the city's gay clubs. The timid may be glad to hear that Thursday is "straight night," but Tracks is not for the timid. Not far from Tracks in Southeast is **The Edge,** a two-dance-floor, six-bar club with live entertainment and an anything-goes atmosphere. By way of explanation: Porn star Ty Fox was a recent guest bartender.

D.C.'s lesbian community has no similarly over-the-top nightspots. There are far more weekly and monthly "Women's Nights" in town—the newest at **Ozone**—than there are actual lesbian clubs. Of the latter there are exactly two: venerable **Phase One,** a low-key pool-table-and-cigarette-smoke kind of place in Southeast, and the weekends-only **Hung Jury** downtown, whose rowdier, younger patrons crowd a big dance floor. (DJs spin records at both clubs.) You're more likely to see men at Phase One or the Hung Jury than you are to see women at Badlands or Cobalt—though the Hung Jury does forbid entry to males unless they are accompanied by a woman.

What's so funny?... As you might expect, Washington is home to its share—perhaps more than its share—of political humorists. Topical (and, too often, not so topical) comedy revues tend to be sustained indefinitely by the area's steady influx of tourists. Gross National Product does political comedy revues with titles like "Mock the Vote" and "Hell to the Chief" at the **Bayou,** a traditional cement-floored, black-walled rock venue. The Capitol Steps troupe, known for including actual Hill staffers in its ranks, specializes in musical political satire, performed dinner-theater-style on weekends at **Chelsea's,** a tony Georgetown club that features exotic international music the rest of the week. If you've already heard enough Bob Packwood jokes to last a lifetime, catch a Comedy Sportz performance at **The Fun**

Factory, a onetime retail space in an Alexandria strip mall. This improvisational troupe relies heavily on audience participation for an improv show that's structured like a sports event, complete with a referee to cut short languishing bits. Downtown, the **Improv** comedy club, an outpost of the national chain, is the only venue in town for big-name comedians. You'll recognize the interior of this place from Comedy Central.

For the college crowd... As you might expect, most nightspots that are readily identifiable as college hangouts are bars (see The Bar Scene) rather than clubs; a nocturnal stroll down Georgetown's M Street is all it takes to find out where the kids are hanging. If you went to college in Washington, chances are you spent at least one drunken evening lugging somebody's amp or drum kit into the **Grog & Tankard,** a cavelike Wisconsin Avenue bar that has long been a forum for musicians who previously headlined in their parents' basements. The eclectic U Street newcomer **Kaffa House,** which was started up by an entrepreneurial Howard student, draws a boho college crowd. It serves decent Jamaican food, hosts poetry readings, and features, among other things, a weekly open mike for hip-hop DJs in its living-room-scale performance space.

For Gen Xers... In the Maryland suburb of Wheaton is **Phantasmagoria,** a combination record store (for those releases you won't find at Tower), eatery, and local indie-pop showcase. (Find them on the Web at http://www.phantasmagoria.com). The atmosphere is wholesome without being cloying: All its shows start early so that patrons can take the Metro home, and no smoking is allowed. The store, whose performance space is set among bins of new and used records, caters to the plastic-barrette and teeny-backpack crowd—and followers of local music, be they hip or otherwise. **Asylum,** an edgy rock club in Adams-Morgan, is now on its third location, this one following a stint on U Street, during which it called itself Asylum in Exile. (Asylum was known as a grunge hangout during that music's heyday, but seems to have recovered nicely.) The new club is tucked under a Pizza Movers in a basement space that was once a vegan restaurant staffed by robed Buddhists; perhaps due to that lingering vibe, its new menu is rife with vegetarian options. Down the block, **Crush,** a spacious two-story club, announces its presence with a sleek pink neon sign. A self-described "cocktail lounge and nightspot," Crush is a good place to verify at least one hot Gen-X trend: People are drinking better as opposed to more. (Ten years ago, this crowd would have been listening to Springsteen and drinking Bud; now it's techno and cosmopolitans.) Crush's name was well chosen; it's elbow-to-elbow with young scene-makers on weekend nights.

For 30-somethings... Nothing soothes aging nerves like staring at the fish tank behind the bar at **Chief Ike's Mambo Room** for a few hours. The bar and dance space—dominated by a large wall mural of Dwight D. Eisenhower in a Native American headdress, grinning and straddling a missile—enjoyed a brief vogue at the start of Clinton's first term, when there was a minor media frenzy over what exactly all the city's hip young Democrats were doing at night. Then and now it draws a defiantly unfashionable crowd put off by Ike's trendier Adams-Morgan neighbors. Refreshingly low-key **Iota**—whose name was originally intended to reflect its cramped quarters but which has since expanded exponentially—is the perfect low-lights-and-exposed-brick backdrop for local rock, blues, and country acts. In addition to established names, the club hosts bands that are, in the heartfelt words of one longtime scenester, "new without being terrible." Iota has considerable appeal to those old enough to want to see live music somewhere that you can a) sit down and b) carry on a conversation.

For 40- and 50-somethings... Once upon a time the over-40 crowd congregated at the River Club, a luxury Georgetown nightspot so classy it had live big-band music and free cigars in the men's room. (Its catty local nickname? "The Liver Club"—as in spots.) But the Liver, uh, River Club closed its Art Deco doors this year, which leaves the field to the **Yacht Club of Bethesda.** This suburban Maryland nightspot in the basement of a Holiday Inn is the dance club of choice among suburban Washington's older singles—and not the kind of singles who relish the experience. Owner and emcee Tommy Curtis, a longtime D.C. promoter, tirelessly flogs the club's reputation as a source of subsequent mates. Call him Cupid in a leisure suit.

For the AARP set... An old banquet hall on Route 175 near Jessup, Maryland, **Max Blob's Bavarian Biergarten and Polka Palace** is *the* place to go for your 70th birthday party. The space is big and dark with lofty rafters like the inside of a barn and long tables situated around a dance floor. The kitchen serves German-style food and the band plays old standards—and, of course, polkas. The crowd will line-dance to anything—including, according to one eyewitness, the Clash's "Rock the Casbah." Sort of like crashing a wedding reception for people you don't know, a visit to Blob's is a great sociological adventure for a group.

Latin conjugations... Downtown's **Coco Loco** is an upscale Brazilian restaurant that becomes a dance club when they clear the tables. Salsa, merengue, and samba predominate, but Coco Loco is just campy enough to spin "The Macarena" once or twice. The club attracts a flamboyant international crowd. At **Habana Village** in Adams-Morgan, an unpretentious neighborhood joint, you can take salsa lessons, or you can just get tutored informally by the outgoing regulars. **Diversite,** where a balcony looms low over the dance floor, plays Argentinian and Cuban music for an urbane downtown clientele. Were it not for, say, the Monday-night tango lessons, it could pass for an Art Deco supper club. Ever-festive **Escándalo!** is a gay Latin dance club where people of all kinds come for attractions that range from drag shows to merengue lessons. The decor is southwestern kitsch—think chili peppers and cacti.

Adams-Morgan extremes... In addition to its weekend parking gridlock, Northwest's Adams-Morgan neighborhood is known for its eclectic mix of restaurants and clubs. All are in close proximity to one another along a two-block stretch of 18th Street, making door-to-door sampling relatively painless. The sprawling **Cities** is distinguished by what may be D.C.'s most elaborate gimmick: Every few years, it closes down and redecorates in the likeness of a different major city, with the cuisine changing accordingly (it's currently Istanbul). There's dancing upstairs Thursday through Saturday, and a crowd composed largely of chain-smoking urban sophisticates. Close by is the multi-storied restaurant and sometime nightclub **Felix,** a converted town house that has the ugliest facade in Washington. With its main floor dominated by a mural depicting a jumbled city skyline, Felix hosts not one but two of the area's increasingly prevalent cigar-and-martini parties on Wednesdays and Saturdays. There is also extensive—and cautionary—mural work in the murky downstairs bar of **Heaven & Hell;** a celestial theme applies upstairs, with angels dangling over the busy dance floor. **Madam's Organ** (the name's a spoonerism for Adams-Morgan) is a smoky hole in the wall with live music most nights and endearing idiosyncrasies such as half-price beer for redheads. "Sorry we're open," reads the sign on the door. Jazz bistro **Cafe Lautrec** features a uniquely weird special attraction on weekends: bar-top tap dancing by local legend Johne Forges. Isn't it the patrons who are supposed to end up doing this? During salsa breaks at the Latin dance club **Habana Village,** make time to read the comments and poetry—in English and Spanish—that patrons write in magic marker on the dismantled orange crates covering the walls.

Go-go and dancehall... The **Capital City Pavilion** is the city's preeminent go-go venue. At this writing, local favorites the Backyard Band perform there on Fridays, Rare Essence on Saturdays. All shows are "all ages" at this big, clean hall on Georgia Avenue, NW; no smoking or drinking is allowed. Patrons are curious about outsiders, but not unfriendly. Due to the violence that has plagued area go-go venues in the past, elaborate security measures are enforced—shoes are removed and examined, and it's not unusual for women to take off their underwire bras so they won't set off the metal detector. The music is loud and the dancing raunchy. At the back of the hall, photographers take portraits of patrons in front of their choice of painted backdrops. **Deno's**, in northeast D.C., is not as safe for the uninitiated as the Capital City Pavilion (except on weekend afternoons, when it features "hand-dancing," an indigenous style of couples dancing that is so locally specialized it has different steps corresponding to different parts of the city). The small stage at Deno's—formerly Breeze's Metro Room, which looms large in local music history—has been the site of many definitive go-go recordings, such as Chuck Brown's "Live at Breeze's Metro Room."

Whatever happened to...? **Bayou,** situated near the Georgetown waterfront, is a narrow, two-level club whose second-floor balcony rings the floor below; the high stage and small, open floor famously puts viewers eye-to-shoe with their favorite acts. One of the hottest things going throughout most of the eighties, this club no longer books many of the city's big-name rock shows, though the rather clueless young crowd that gathers here doesn't seem to care. The club hasn't yet managed to establish a new identity, but it does seem to be the venue of choice for declining metal acts, a bit like the club equivalent of a second-run movie theater. The Next Step, a Grateful Dead tribute band, plays here on Mondays; the Gross National Product comedy troupe on Saturdays. **Jaxx** in Springfield, Virginia, caters specifically to the "Where are they now?" market. Recent headliners included such classic rock relics as Foghat and the Marshall Tucker Band. Expect to find a mall-metal crowd congregating here; the club hosts a lot of battle-of-the-bands marathons and all-ages shows. Hair-whipping is a must.

Bare necessities... There is, both literally and figuratively, no cover at **The Royal Palace,** a strip club prominently positioned at a Connecticut Avenue intersection north of Dupont Circle. But that doesn't mean you'll get off cheap. This overpriced nightclub—or "ight Club," as the sign on the door reads—is a big draw for out-of-towners, perhaps in part because it's only a block away from the so-called Hinkley Hilton. Georgetown's **Good Guys** is where you'll find beer-soaked locals and a smattering of titillated college kids—it's conveniently located between Georgetown and American University. Inside, it's about as respectable as you can expect a strip club to be. Like a perverse cross between a fire station and a gym, its three stages are equipped with floor-to-ceiling poles and chin-up bars. More high profile is **Archibald's,** whose shared location with Fanatics Sports Bar (see The Bar Scene) forces patrons to choose between naked women and televised sports. Some have never recovered. The club's ubiquitous golden fliers, which blanket the downtown area like autumn leaves, proclaim the entertainment the "best damn girlie show in town." It almost goes without saying that the club's information number is 202/737–BOOB; a call will get you the names of that day's dancers.

A little bit country... Alexandria's **Birchmere** may be the most agreeable place in the Washington area to watch live music—and not simply because they serve cheese fries. An added incentive to visit is the variety and quality of local and national country and folk artists—with some subdued rockers thrown into the mix—that pass through this understated music club. It's arranged dinner-theater-style with tables facing a small stage. Tabletop signs ("Shhhh!") enjoin patrons to be silent while music is in progress. If only real life were like this. Bethesda's **Twist & Shout** is a mostly zydeco and Cajun club immortalized by hometown girl Mary Chapin Carpenter in her 1990 hit "Down at the Twist & Shout." Since then, the club has survived a couple of name and location changes; it's now housed in the Bethesda American Legion Hall, a thematically appropriate setting for its roster of down-home acts. The best of Louisiana takes to its floor-level stage, as do local regulars like rockabilly guitarist Bill Kirchen and his band Too Much Fun. An area mainstay in his own right, Kirchen is a veteran of the late-sixties country-rock outfit Commander Cody and His Lost Planet Airmen, a group best—and, indeed, only—remembered for the 1971 novelty hit "Hot Rod Lincoln."

Retrogression... You may think the retro craze is over, but in Washington, where trends tend to arrive a few years too late (sorry, we were all busy watching the "MacNeil-Lehrer News Hour"), it is in full swing. At the rate retro nights are popping up around town, it won't be long before the Library of Congress is the only place in town you can go without being expected to do the Hustle. Upstairs at **Heaven & Hell,** a three-story town house in club-choked Adams-Morgan, there is a perennially popular eighties dance party on Thursdays; the line stretches down the block. (In Hell, which is, of course, downstairs, there's no room to dance.) **Polly Esther's,** the latest on the retro-kitsch bandwagon, hosts a "Charlie's Angels" Night. The seventies are downstairs and the eighties upstairs at this memorabilia-plastered time capsule of a club; you haven't seen so many Barbies and Erik Estrada posters since your high-school bedroom. (Cutesy theme drinks include the Ghostbuster and the Alex P. Keaton.) At **Decades,** which takes over all five floors of the Ritz on Friday nights, separate floors feature music from the seventies, eighties, and nineties. (Overheard on the stairs: "All the girls like the seventies, but the guys like the eighties.") As part of a long-running promotion, contestants for MTV's "Singled Out" were chosen here. Enough said. Dupont Circle's **Childe Harold** restaurant becomes the Step Childe on Friday and Saturday nights, a dance club featuring seventies and eighties music.

For insomniacs... Things don't get started until late at the **Capital City Pavilion,** but they last all night. The club's recorded message says it all: It's open "from 11pm till you're tired and want to go." Several clubs stop serving alcohol at the appointed hour, but stay open for a soda-chugging after-hours dance crowd: You'll find an industrial dance mix and fashion victims veiled in cigarette smoke at **Ozone;** a gay crowd dancing to top-volume disco at **Cobalt;** club kids grooving to house in chunky platform shoes at **Red;** and nonstop K.C. and the Sunshine Band at **Decades.** As usual, the ravers best everyone else when it comes to staying up past their bedtimes. Friday night's "Buzz" at the **Capitol Ballroom,** which draws thousands of raver types each week, lasts from 10pm until 8am. Still looking for something to do? See Late Night Dining for places that serve breakfast.

The Club Scene: Index

Note: If no Metro stop is listed, a club is best reached by taxi or car. The nearest Metro stop to Georgetown is Foggy Bottom-GWU, a 15-minute walk or short cab ride away.

9:30 Club The District's foremost midsize venue for national rock acts.... *Tel 202/393–0930. 815 V St., NW. Cover. U Street–Cardozo Metro.* **(see pp. 26, 27)**

Archibald's. Here all male fantasies converge; sports on TV, beer on tap, naked girls on stage.... *Tel 202/737–2662. 1520 K St., NW. No cover. Farragut North Metro.* **(see p. 37)**

Asylum. Basement-level alt-rock hangout in Adams-Morgan.... *Tel 202/319–9353. 2471 18th St., NW. Cover. Woodley Park–Zoo Metro.* **(see p. 33)**

Badlands. A closer-to-home alternative to Tracks, this crowded Dupont Circle dance club marks the western end of the gay nightclubber's P Street circuit.... *Tel 202/296–0505. 1413 22nd St., NW. Closed Mon–Wed. Cover. Dupont Circle Metro.* **(see p. 31)**

The Bank. Platform-dance in a fog of dry ice at this dance space in what was once a downtown bank.... *Tel 202/737–3177. 915 F St., NW. Closed Mon–Wed. Cover. Gallery Place–Chinatown Metro.* **(see p. 30)**

Bayou. High eighties Georgetown rock club; hosts performances by the Gross National Product comedy troupe most Saturdays.... *Tel 202/333–2897. 3135 K St., NW. Cover.* **(see pp. 32, 37)**

Birchmere. Unpretentious country and folk venue—note the red-and-white checked vinyl tablecloths. Books a mix of local and national acts.... *Tel 703/549–5919. 3901 Mount Vernon Ave., Alexandria, VA. Closed Sun–Mon. Cover.* **(see p. 38)**

Black Cat. Hip concert club with adjacent bar is a showcase for local and national indie acts.... *Tel 202/667–7960. 1831 14th St., NW. Cover. U Street–Cardozo Metro.* **(see p. 27)**

Blues Alley. As atmospheric as it is pricey, the choice jazz venue in town—you'll sit 5 feet away from the best names in jazz.... *Tel 202/337–4141. 1073 Wisconsin Ave., NW. (Enter through alley south of M St. and Wisconsin Ave.) Cover and drink minimums.* **(see p. 30)**

Cafe Lautrec. Faux French bistro with live jazz and bar-top tap dancing.... *Tel 202/265–6436. 2431 18th St., NW. No cover; food and drink minimums. Woodley Park–Zoo Metro.* **(see pp. 31, 36)**

Capital City Pavilion. Washington's best go-go shows; best come late and unarmed.... *Tel 202/722–0994. 3401 Georgia Ave., NW. Cover.* **(see p. 36)**

Capitol Ballroom. This sprawling warehouse space is both rock venue and dance club.... *Tel 202/554–1500. Half St. at K St., SE. Cover. Navy Yard Metro.* **(see pp. 27, 30, 39)**

The Cellar. Showy underground disco packed with coeds looking to score.... *Tel 202/457–8180. 2100 M St., NW. Closed Mon–Wed. Cover. Foggy Bottom–GWU Metro.* **(see p. 30)**

Chelsea's. Hosts the political comedy troupe Capitol Steps; tickets are pricey and the dress code forbids tennis shoes.... *Tel 202/298–8222 for reservations. 1055 Thomas Jefferson St., NW. Capitol Steps perform Fri–Sat.* **(see p. 32)**

Chief Ike's Mambo Room. Sticky-floored beer joint has a small dance floor and a certain roguish charm.... *Tel 202/332–2211. 1725 Columbia Rd., NW. Cover on weekends. Woodley Park–Zoo Metro.* **(see p. 34)**

Childe Harold. Landmark Dupont Circle restaurant and bar becomes Step Childe, a retro dance club, on weekends.... *Tel 202/483-6700. 1610 20th St., NW. Cover. Dupont Circle Metro.* **(see p. 39)**

The Circle. Mainstream neon-and-chrome gay nightclub welcomes a mix of races and gender preferences for drinking and dancing.... *Tel 202/462-5575. 1629 Connecticut Ave., NW. Cover. Dupont Circle Metro.* **(see p. 32)**

Cities. Fashionable Adams-Morgan restaurant and bar theoretically has dancing on weekends, but it's much too crowded to say for sure.... *Tel 202/328-7195. 2424 18th St., NW. Dance club open Thur–Sat. Cover for club only. Woodley Park–Zoo Metro.* **(see p. 35)**

City Blues Cafe. Local blues acts perform in the bay window of this Woodley Park town-house restaurant and bar.... *Tel 202/232-2300. 2651 Connecticut Ave., NW. Cover; no cover for diners. Woodley Park Metro.* **(see p. 31)**

Club Zei. Overpriced, overdecorated, and overloud Zei may constitute the quintessential nightclub experience.... *Tel 202/842-2445. 1415 Zei Alley, between H and I sts., NW. Closed Sun–Wed. Cover. McPherson Square Metro.* **(see pp. 22, 26, 29)**

Cobalt. Stylish gay dance club off Dupont Circle... *Tel 202/797-0560. 1639 R St., NW. Cover. Dupont Circle Metro.* **(see pp. 31, 39)**

Coco Loco. Thronged by the best-dressed clientele in the city, this Brazilian restaurant becomes a high-energy merengue palace Thursday through Saturday.... *Tel 202/289-2626. 810 7th St., NW. Cover. Gallery Place–Chinatown Metro.* **(see p. 35)**

Crush. ...or be crushed at this popular new addition to the Adams-Morgan nightlife scene.... *Tel 202/319-1111. 2323 18th St., NW. Cover on weekends. Woodley Park–Zoo Metro.* **(see p. 34)**

Decades. A big attraction for the fake-ID crowd, this Fridays-only club features music from the sixties, seventies, and

eighties on different floors.... *Tel 703/242–3648. 919 E St., NW. Fri only. Cover. Gallery Place–Chinatown Metro.*
(see p. 39)

Deno's. Longtime home to D.C.'s home-grown go-go.... *Tel 202/526–8880. 2335 Bladensburg Rd., NE. Cover.*
(see p. 36)

Diversité. Near the Woolly Mammoth and Studio theaters; cosmopolitan restaurant and nightclub specializing in Argentinean and Cuban music.... *Tel 202/234–5740. 1526 14th St., NW. Cover. Dupont Circle Metro.*
(see p. 35)

The Edge. Vast gay club houses multiple bars, multiple dance floors, and multiple patrons.... *Tel 202/488–1200. 52 L St., SE. Cover.*
(see p. 32)

Eighteenth Street Lounge. Candlelit acid-jazz/house/bossa-nova lounge with an exclusive door policy on weekends.... *Tel 202/466–3922. 1212 18th St., NW. Closed Sun. Cover on weekends. Farragut North Metro.*
(see pp. 22, 28)

Escándalo! High-energy gay dance club with a Latin flavor draws everyone from drag queens to squares.... *Tel 202/822–8909. 2122 P St., NW. Cover. Dupont Circle Metro.*
(see pp. 31, 35)

Felix. Modernistic eyesore of a restaurant whose multiple personalities include a dance club and a martini lounge.... *Tel 202/483–3549. 2406 18th St., NW. Closed Sun. No cover. Woodley Park–Zoo Metro.*
(see p. 36)

The Fraternity House. This late night gay pickup spot is located in the alley between 21st and 22nd Sts... *Tel 202/223–4917. 2122 P St. rear, NW. Cover. Open Mon until 3 am; Tue–Wed & Sun until 2 am; Thur until 4 am; Fri–Sat until 5 am. Dupont Circle Metro.*
(see p. 31)

The Fun Factory. Suburban storefront that the improvisational comedy troupe Comedy Sportz calls home.... *Tel 703/684–5212. 3112 Mt. Vernon Ave., Alexandria, VA. Cover.*
(see p. 32)

Good Guys. Rare is the D.C. native who doesn't have a story about trying to sneak into this Glover Park girlie bar as a teenager.... *Tel 202/338–8128. 2311 Wisconsin Ave., NW. No cover.* **(see p. 37)**

Grog & Tankard. Legendarily unprepossessing collegiate watering hole and first-gig site of amateur bands.... *Tel 202/333–3114. 2408 Wisconsin Ave., NW. Cover.* **(see p. 33)**

Habana Village. Everybody's your best friend at this Latin dance club where the merengue is liable to suddenly become mandatory.... *Tel 202/462–6310. 1834 Columbia Rd., NW. Closed Sun–Tue. Cover includes free drink. Woodley Park–Zoo Metro.* **(see pp. 35, 36)**

Heaven & Hell. Like the latter, it can be loud, dark, and crowded, especially on weekends.... *Tel 703/522–4227. 2327 18th St., NW. Closed Sun–Mon. Cover. Woodley Park–Zoo Metro.* **(see pp. 36, 38)**

Hung Jury. Men are only admitted as the guests of female patrons at this affably rowdy lesbian bar and dance club.... *Tel 202/279–3212. 1819 H St., NW. Open Fri–Sat. Cover. Farragut West Metro.* **(see p. 32)**

Improv. Showcase for national stand-up acts with the ambience of an airport lounge.... *Tel 202/296–7008. 1140 Connecticut Ave., NW. Cover. Farragut North Metro.* **(see p. 33)**

Iota. Understated restaurant and club features local musicians and a markedly genial staff.... *Tel 703/522–8340. 2832 Wilson Blvd., Arlington, VA. Cover. Clarendon Metro.* **(see p. 34)**

Jaxx. Where seventies AM radio comes alive. Sort of.... *Tel 703/569–5940. 6355 Rolling Rd., Springfield, VA. Cover.* **(see p. 37)**

Kaffa House. Dedicated to the dissemination of African coffee and local prosody.... *Tel 202/462–1212. 1212 U St., NW. Cover. U Street–Cardozo Metro.* **(see p. 33)**

Madam's Organ. A pleasantly down-at-heel vibe and live blues are among the attractions at this neighborhood haunt.... *Tel 202/667–5370. 2461 18th St., NW. Cover on weekends. Woodley Park–Zoo Metro.* **(see pp. 31, 36)**

Max Blob's Bavarian Biergarten and Polka Palace. There aren't many places these days where you can polka to "The Electric Slide" without irony.... *Tel 410/799–0155. 8024 Blob's Park Rd., Jessup, MD. Cover.* **(see p. 35)**

New Vegas Lounge. You are the guest of proprietor Dr. Blues at what many consider the city's most authentic blues joint; but please, no tennis shoes.... *Tel 202/483–3971. 1415 P St., NW. Closed Sun–Mon. Cover. Dupont Circle Metro.* **(see p. 31)**

One Step Down. Unobtrusive Pennsylvania Avenue jazz venue.... *Tel 202/331–8863. 2517 Pennsylvania Ave., NW. Cover and drink minimums. Foggy Bottom–GWU Metro.* **(see p. 30)**

Ozone. Trendy multilevel dance club so affected it has a subtitle: "Le Club Industriel."... *Tel 202/293–0303. 1214 18th St., NW. Closed Sun and Tue. Cover. Farragut North Metro.* **(see pp. 29, 32, 39)**

Phantasmagoria. Cool little record store that's also a restaurant and local music showcase.... *Tel 301/949–8886. 11319 Elkin St., Wheaton, MD. Cover. Wheaton Metro.* **(see p. 33)**

Phase One. Capitol Hill lesbian club that one regular terms "older than God."... *Tel 202/544–6831. 525 8th St., SE. Cover on weekends. Capitol South Metro.* **(see p. 32)**

Planet Fred. With planets descending from the ceiling and lava lamps bolted to the wall, this dance club is determinedly zany.... *Tel 202/466–2336. 1221 Connecticut Ave., NW. Cover on weekends. Farragut North Metro.* **(see p. 30)**

Polly Esther's. Situated, its print ads point out, "between F for Funky and G for Groovy streets," this seventies/eighties dance club is neither.... *Tel 202/737–1970. 605 12th St., NW. Closed Sun–Tue. Cover. Metro Center.* **(see p. 38)**

Red. Minimalist late-night dance club where scenesters end up after everything else closes.... *Tel 202/466–3475. 1802 Jefferson Pl., NW. Cover. Farragut North Metro.* **(see pp. 29, 39)**

Republic Gardens. A cosmopolitan crowd—and we do mean crowd—has made this the club of the moment. Literally stops traffic on U Street on weekends.... *Tel 202/232–2710. 1355 U St., NW. Cover. U Street–Cardozo Metro.* **(see p. 28)**

Ritz. Sprawling multilevel club, said to be the largest in town, features a mix of jazz, reggae, and hip-hop in its five sections.... *Tel 202/638–2582. 919 E St., NW. Cover. Gallery Place–Chinatown Metro.* **(see p. 28)**

The Royal Palace. Dupont Circle strip club known for its high drink prices and boisterous crowds, a combination you'd think would be mutually exclusive.... *Tel 202/462–2623. 1805 Connecticut Ave., NW. No cover. Dupont Circle Metro.* **(see p. 37)**

Spy Club. In addition to its alley location, the Spy Club shares its dress code and high cover charge with neighboring Club Zei.... *Tel 202/289–1779. 805 15th St., between H and I sts., NW. Closed Sun–Wed. Cover. McPherson Square Metro.* **(see pp. 22, 29)**

State of the Union. Years after the collapse of the Soviet Union, this eclectic Lenin-themed club is still the place to be for reggae fans, acid jazzers, and U Street scene-makers.... *Tel 202/588–8810. 1357 U St., NW. Cover. U Street–Cardozo Metro.* **(see pp. 26, 28)**

Tracks. The mother ship of D.C. nightclubs, this rambling, gay-owned space draws gays and straights alike and—in a city of nightclub superlatives—boasts the largest dance floor on the East Coast.... *Tel 202/488–3320. 1111 1st St., SE. Closed Mon–Wed. Cover.* **(see pp. 26, 29, 32)**

Twist & Shout. Unremarkable setting in an American Legion Hall where a remarkable array of country, zydeco, and Cajun artists perform.... *Tel 301/652–3383. 4800 Auburn Ave., Bethesda, MD. Cover. Bethesda Metro.* **(see p. 38)**

Yacht Club of Bethesda. Home of the over-50 singles scene.... *Tel 301/654–2396. 8111 Woodmont Ave., Bethesda, MD. Closed Sun–Mon. Cover. Bethesda Metro.* **(see p. 34)**

the bar

scene 2

Washington Confidential, Jack Lait and Lee Mortimer's 1950 sleazography of the nation's capital, speculates that "the first question asked by members of the new

Seventh Congress, after taking the oath in the draughty and unfinished Capitol in 1801, was 'where is a saloon with dames?' or the early 19th-century equivalent thereof." And things haven't changed that much since.

Even earlier, in 1791, George Washington planned his eponymous city-to-be at Suter's Tavern in Georgetown (in the 1000 block of Wisconsin Avenue, NW)—a joint so popular that it later provided temporary digs for the House of Representatives. During the Civil War, today's bureaucracy-filled Federal Triangle (Pennsylvania Avenue, Constitution Avenue, and 13th Street, NW) was a seedy nightlife district known as "Hooker's Division" after the troops of General Joseph Hooker, who frequented its establishments. The division is long gone, but ladies of the evening are still known by the name bestowed as a result of their association with Hooker and his boys.

Washington's oldest existing bar (founded in 1856) is the Old Ebbitt Grill (see Late Night Dining), which, at various downtown locations, has set 'em up for future presidents Grant, Cleveland, McKinley, and T. Roosevelt. (As a Georgetown undergrad, Bill Clinton's chosen hangout was The Tombs.)

In a doomed effort to reverse the alcoholic tide, a teetotaling dentist named Henry Cogswell gave the city the oddly magnificent Temperance Fountain in 1880, which still stands—but doesn't flow—at the corner of 7th Street and Pennsylvania Avenue, NW. But Washington found yet another reason to party upon the arrival of Prohibition, as evidenced by the career of bootlegger David D. Davenport, his record 115 court appearances in one year proving how good business must have been.

Reborn legal in the 1930s, bars flourished during World War II, when the huge infusion of war workers went out nightly to escape their overcrowded apartments. During the 1960s and 1970s, D.C.'s 18-year-old beer-drinking age turned Georgetown into a magnet for thirsty students from states near and distant. (The legal age is now 21, like everywhere else.) Tawdry nightlife also used to flourish along the 14th Street Corridor, where a younger, friskier Mayor Marion Barry reportedly frequented a joint called This Is It, and a stripper at the Silver Slipper nightclub, Fanne Foxe, met Congressman Wilbur Mills (D-AR), the influential (and married) chairman of the Ways and Means Committee, for a moonlight tour of Potomac Park. (After police stopped them to protest Mills' fast-track, middle-of-the-road position on nocturnal motoring, Foxe plunged into the Tidal Basin in a futile attempt to save the congressman's reputation.)

Though 14th Street has become more businesslike and boringly respectable, the Washington bar scene continues to thrive in Georgetown, Dupont Circle, U Street, Capitol Hill, Adams-Morgan, and Alexandria Old Town—although things haven't been quite the same since Ted Kennedy remarried. Bars are a significant social factor in this deal-cutting town: You may not find a place where everybody knows your name, but odds are you'll find one where everybody knows which congressman you staff for.

Of course, no establishment calls itself a "bar" anymore. Gone is the *Lost Weekend*–style smoky tavern with one long bar where a man in a rumpled fedora sits as a time-lapse sequence reveals the steady accumulation of empty glasses at his elbow. Don't bother looking under "bars" in the D.C. Yellow Pages—the listings jump directly from "bar coding" to "bar fixtures." (Admittedly, the latter category does seem to imply the existence of bars, but nobody's committing themselves.) Even granting that it's less acceptable these days to go out explicitly to get hammered—though the practice is catching on again with 20-somethings—this coyness seems especially pertinent to D.C., where everybody zealously tailors their public appearance. A Washington bar is never just a bar; it's always a restaurant or a club or concert hall or a pool hall. Given this blurring of nightlife boundaries, bear in mind that what were called bars in simpler times may also be listed in this book under Clubs or Late Night Dining.

Whatever the nomenclature, there are still plenty of places that fulfill the prerequisites of a good bar. What are they? Lighting and seating can make or break a bar's ambiance; specifically, you don't want too much of the former or not enough of the latter. Booze factors into the equation, of course. And music. Most Washington bars feature local performers, many of whom are outstanding. Bar entertainment, though, shouldn't be the kind that makes conversation an impossibility. As author Quentin Crisp has observed, "No one is interesting when he's shouting."

D.C. bars tend to reflect the discrete factions of the population: pols, college kids, tourists, and native Washingtonians (yes, some do exist). These are the subgroups of Washington's citizenry, and like herd animals, they tend to migrate in groups.

The Beaten Path

If tourists know nothing else about nightlife in Washington, they know from **Georgetown.** There, they join window-shopping teens, college students stumbling from bar to bar, military guys in buzz cuts and pressed polo shirts, and internationals babbling into cell phones. In short, you won't see many regular—whatever that means—Washingtonians here. Georgetown has a fair quotient of quasi-historic kitsch, but don't expect Main Street U.S.A.—here you might actually step in curbside vomit, or create some yourself. The bars in Georgetown are chockablock, wedged between the bookstores and eateries, and, because they're aimed at the universal tourist demographic, seem interchangeable. And when you consider that there's no Georgetown Metro stop (the nearest is Foggy Bottom–GWU) and on-street parking is next to impossible to find, Georgetown's charms become even less exciting.

Dupont Circle is more or less the epicenter of Washington nightlife; it has a Metro station and cabs galore, and its radiating side streets cover a wide geographic—and demographic—territory. Dupont Circle is the heart of Washington's gay scene, but that exists side by side with bars for cruising straight singles, happy-hour revelers, and middle-age couples. With so many big hotels nearby, you'll also see a lot of conventioneers proudly proclaiming their beyond-the-Beltway residency by failing to remove their plastic name tags. In the center of the Circle itself is a large fountain ringed by benches; if you don't mind sharing space with attack pigeons, skaters going at the speed of light, bike delivery people who swarm there at sunset, and assorted other loonies, there are worse places to spend a summer evening.

Dupont Circle is a good jumping-off point, not too far from the nightlife-rich neighborhoods of Adams-Morgan and U Street. **Adams-Morgan,** the most recently gentrified of Washington's neighborhoods, has been a nightlife magnet since the late 1970s. Sandwiched between the Ethiopian restaurants and Gen-X clubs are some surprisingly pleasant drinking spots. Nearby **U Street,** specifically the 1200 through 1600 blocks thereof, has few single-use nightspots; most of its bars are in restaurants or clubs where the main attraction is food, dancing, or music. This is the site of D.C.'s freshest, hippest, and most integrated after-dark scene; see it quick before it loses its edge. In contrast, there's nothing but bars on **Capitol Hill;** they are concentrated along

Pennsylvania Avenue, SE, and in the vicinity of Union Station. Because this is an area where people come, by and large, to work—and perhaps because it's not especially safe at night—the Hill has few restaurants and fewer clubs, but the bars are packed at lunch and during happy hour.

Tired of D.C. already? Cross under the Potomac on Metro or drive over Key Bridge to Wilson Boulevard in **Arlington.** Don't be alarmed by the city's appalling public art, the most obvious example of which is the huge sculpture near the corner of Wilson Boulevard and North Oak Street, a massive bouquet of huge silver arrows that looks like the logo on a detergent box. Fortunately, things brighten up a little farther down Wilson Boulevard, where a proliferation of clubs, bars, and restaurants support a hopping home-grown night scene. Or head down to **Alexandria,** where King Street, Old Town's main thoroughfare, has a bar every few feet. As its name implies, Old Town is a historic area that occupies the site of Alexandria's once-bustling seaport, the third largest in colonial America. Today, the neighborhood is rife with precious gift shops and self-consciously quaint bars and restaurants. The Alexandria waterfront is a high-profile tourist destination, and many of its bars charge hefty covers as a matter of course. But it's possible to enjoy Old Town without actually going indoors. King Street dead-ends at the water, where riverfront benches and a pier are open to the public and ubiquitous street performers provide an al fresco background track.

What to Order

At mid-century, quoth *Washington Confidential,* "the most popular kind of liquor [was] bourbon, suh, with rye next. Only...English diplomats, New Yorkers, and spats-wearers drink Scotch." Bourbon is out nowadays, although spats-wearers and their ilk have not prevailed: the closest thing to a Washington house drink is a microbrew, with a slight preference for local brands Olde Heurich lager (named after the brewery demolished to make way for Kennedy Center) and Foggy Bottom Ale. Typically, since Washington manufactures almost nothing but words, these flavorsome concoctions are produced by a brewery in Utica, New York. Microbrews, however, have lost their cachet lately (see What's Hot, What's Not), being replaced by cosmopolitans, martinis, and other mixed drinks.

Etiquette

Drinkers in D.C. must be over 21, and most bars and nightclubs routinely card patrons. Some venues admit under-21 patrons sans drinking privileges, marking them with hand stamps or wristbands. (But don't count on it. Call ahead to ask the policy.) District bars are allowed to serve booze until 3am Saturday and Sunday and 2am the rest of the week, which defines the hours of operation for just about all the bars in this chapter. Expect earlier closing times at bars appended to restaurants, like the one at the Tabard Inn, and bars in areas that don't get much nighttime foot traffic, like downtown's Capitol City Brewing Company. A $1 tip for drinks procured at the bar is customary, as is $2 for table service or, if wait staff serve your table round after round, a standard 15% tip. Some places will start a running tab, others will ask that you pay drink by drink. As a rule, table service entails a running tab, while sitting at the bar means you pay as you go. Word to the wise: D.C. is a tough city to drive in while sober. Don't try it drunk.

Adams-Morgan and Dupont Circle Bars

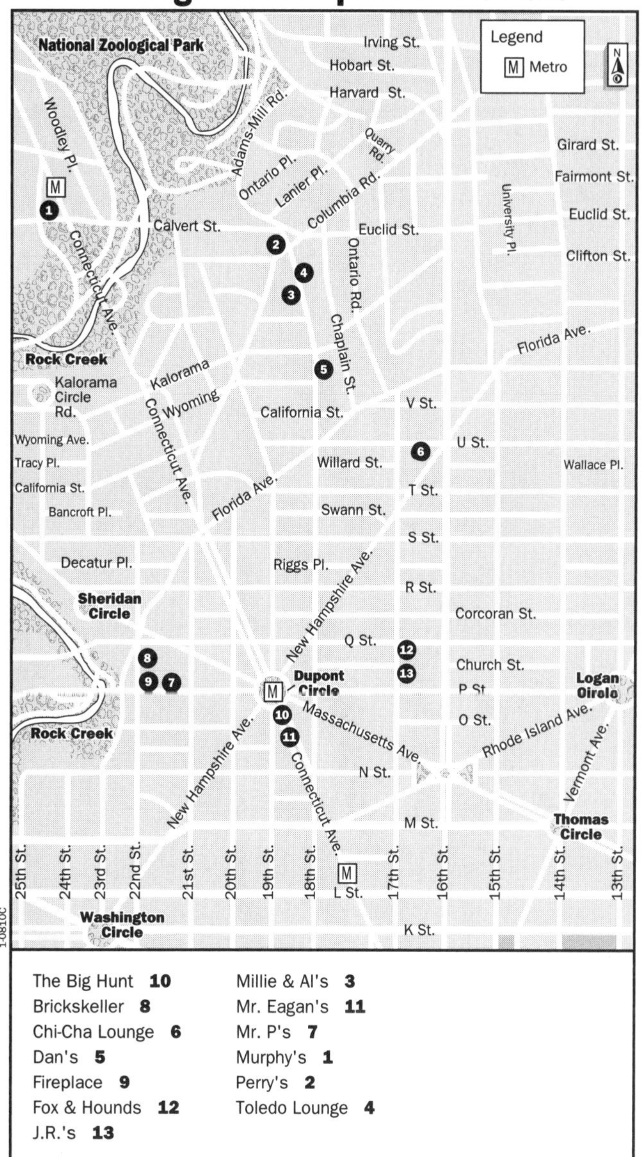

The Big Hunt **10**	Millie & Al's **3**
Brickskeller **8**	Mr. Eagan's **11**
Chi-Cha Lounge **6**	Mr. P's **7**
Dan's **5**	Murphy's **1**
Fireplace **9**	Perry's **2**
Fox & Hounds **12**	Toledo Lounge **4**
J.R.'s **13**	

Georgetown & Downtown Bars

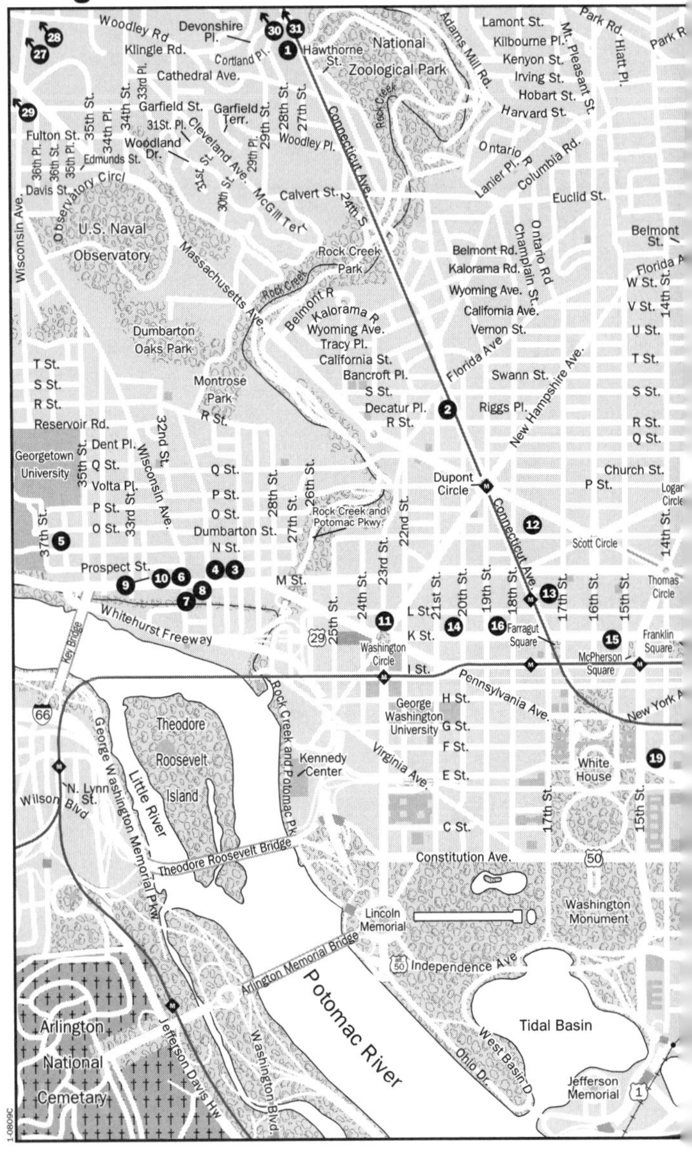

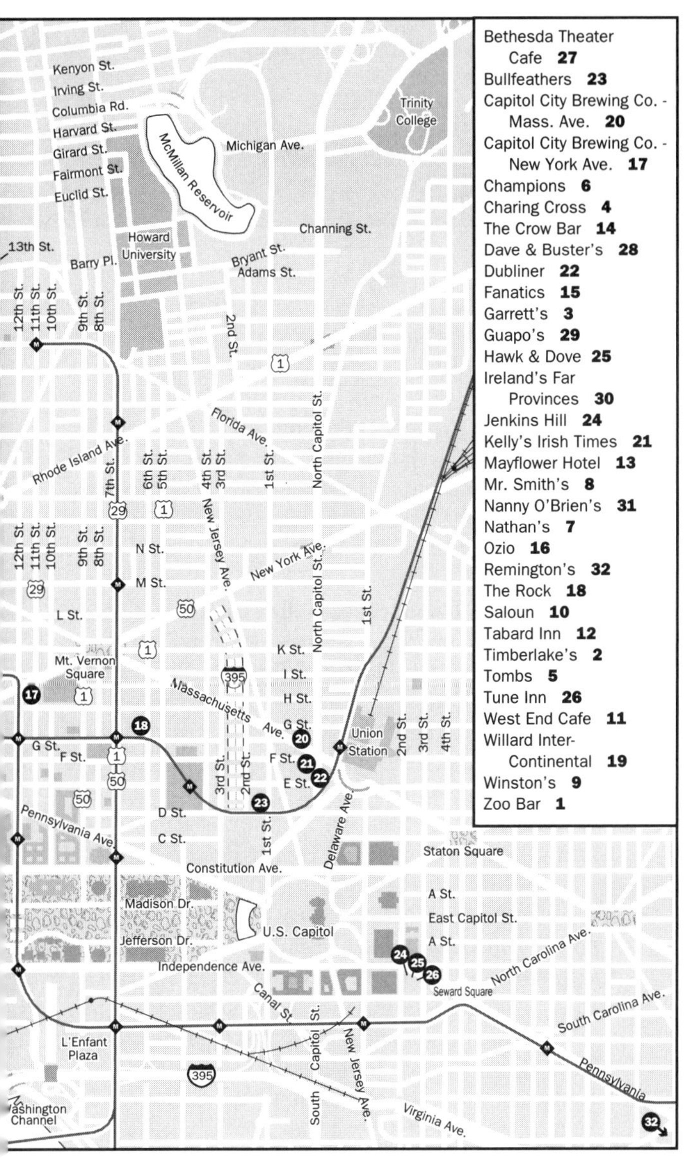
Bethesda Theater Cafe 27
Bullfeathers 23
Capitol City Brewing Co. - Mass. Ave. 20
Capitol City Brewing Co. - New York Ave. 17
Champions 6
Charing Cross 4
The Crow Bar 14
Dave & Buster's 28
Dubliner 22
Fanatics 15
Garrett's 3
Guapo's 29
Hawk & Dove 25
Ireland's Far Provinces 30
Jenkins Hill 24
Kelly's Irish Times 21
Mayflower Hotel 13
Mr. Smith's 8
Nanny O'Brien's 31
Nathan's 7
Ozio 16
Remington's 32
The Rock 18
Saloun 10
Tabard Inn 12
Timberlake's 2
Tombs 5
Tune Inn 26
West End Cafe 11
Willard Inter-Continental 19
Winston's 9
Zoo Bar 1
Kenyon St.
Irving St.
Columbia Rd.
Harvard St.
Girard St.
Fairmont St.
Euclid St.
McMillan Reservoir
Michigan Ave.
Trinity College
Channing St.
Howard University
13th St.
Barry Pl.
Bryant St.
Adams St.
12th St.
11th St.
10th St.
9th St.
8th St.
2nd St.
Florida Ave.
Rhode Island Ave.
7th St.
6th St.
5th St.
4th St.
3rd St.
1st St.
North Capitol St.
New Jersey Ave.
New York Ave.
N St.
M St.
L St.
K St.
I St.
H St.
G St.
F St.
E St.
D St.
C St.
Mt. Vernon Square
Massachusetts Ave.
Union Station
Pennsylvania Ave.
Delaware Ave.
Constitution Ave.
Staton Square
A St.
East Capitol St.
Madison Dr.
Jefferson Dr.
U.S. Capitol
Independence Ave.
North Carolina Ave.
Seward Square
Canal St.
South Capitol St.
South Carolina Ave.
L'Enfant Plaza
Washington Channel
Virginia Ave.
Pennsylvania

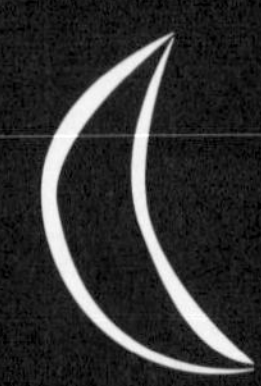

The Lowdown

Political partying... Nightlife in D.C. is strictly nonpartisan—proximity is the single most important factor in determining which bars are favored by which pols. These are people who work a lot, and thus their hangouts are within walking distance of their offices, i.e. Capitol Hill. The House office buildings (Cannon, Rayburn, and Longworth) are south of the Capitol along Independence Avenue; the Senate office buildings (Hart, Dirksen, and Russell) are north of the Capitol along Constitution Avenue. This means that you'll be more likely to find Senators at the **Dubliner** and **Kelly's Irish Times** opposite Union Station, while congressmen bend elbows at Pennsylvania Avenue's **Hawk and Dove** and **Bullfeathers** on 1st Street, SE. Keep in mind that "making the scene" is not high on the priority lists of politicians and their staffers. Of course, if all you want is a place where everybody will be talking politics, just about anywhere in the city will qualify. After all, this is a town where even the house DJ has a position on the Welfare Reform Act.

Where to take a client... There's nowhere better for sedate hobnobbing than the Town & Country Lounge at the **Mayflower Hotel.** The Mayflower dates from 1924; during the twenties, it was the largest hotel in the country. The same firm designed New York's Grand Central Terminal, and every president since Coolidge has attended an inaugural ball in its Grand Ballroom. It's here that you're most likely to run into visiting heads of state in the men's room. Or try the older but less grandiose **Willard Inter-Continental Hotel,** which has two elegant bars: the Round Robin and the Nest. The latter, which dates from the days when women were barred from the Round Robin, hosts live jazz on Friday and Saturday. The hotel (though not the current physical plant) dates from 1816, and in the old days was a residential hotel that housed the likes of Abraham Lincoln. Legend (and Willard p.r.) has it that President Grant coined the word "lobbyists" to describe the political hangers-on who lay in wait in the lobby hoping to buttonhole the lawmakers who lived and socialized here. Those who find the air at the Mayflower and the Willard too rarefied can head across the river to the **Doubletree Hotel,** where the revolving rooftop Skydome Lounge offers a breathtaking view of Washington by night. With sublime subtlety it expresses the primary principle of Washington politics: What goes around comes around.

Best-dressed crowds... At the bar at **Cities** (see The Club Scene), where handsome rattan chairs and open-air decor evoke the exoticism of Istanbul, the $7 you fork over for a cosmopolitan pays for a parade of tanning-bed playboys swathed in Armani. In Adams-Morgan, **Perry's** broad roof deck offers a starry backdrop for long tables full of J. Crew types sharing sushi. U Street's **Chi-Cha Lounge,** a room full of tightly packed, nonmatching chairs and sofas, provides plenty of places to strike up a conversation—or just strike a pose. At the martini-and-cigar lounge **Ozio,** you have to be beautiful or look like Boss Tweed or be too powerful to care if you look ridiculous sauntering among the columns with a fat cigar crammed into your mouth.

Washington's idea of wacky... Though D.C. has no karaoke to speak (or sing) of, it does have **Dave & Buster's,** a 60,000-square-foot glorified carnival arcade for grown-ups. In addition to multiple bars and a full-service restaurant, Dave & Buster's features video games, shuffleboard, pool tables, a dinner theater (see The Arts) and—its most popular attraction—virtual-reality machines. (Under 21s have to be accompanied by adults; no more than three kids per grown-up. Minors are banished after 10pm, though the incidence of childish behavior does not necessarily decrease thereafter.) At both the **Bethesda Theater Cafe** and the **Arlington Cinema and Draft House** you can see recent but pre-videotape movies over pizza and beer. Early in the week at U Street's hipster hangout **Chi-Cha Lounge,** after a carafe of drinks, ask them to bring the hookah over to your big comfy couch and you can toke on flavored tobaccos. The "Beer" totem pole says you've arrived at high-concept **Bardo Rodeo;** look for the CD jukebox embedded in the side of the vintage Plymouth Fury that has seemingly driven through the front window. Out front of the **The Crow Bar** on a Friday evening there's usually a line of Harleys standing at ease; inside, their owners mix it up with K Street lawyers letting down their hair weaves.

When Irish guys are smiling... Look around and you'd swear there are two Irish bars for every Washington resident of Irish extraction. No two Washingtonians, however, agree on which is best. In upper Northwest, **Ireland's Four Provinces** is the area's most congenial Irish bar—inept murals, fake Tiffany lamp shades, and all. Like nearly every Irish bar in town, the Four P's features nightly Irish music—which sometimes means strictly traditional and sometimes a guy with a guitar doing covers of "Brown-Eyed Girl." Across Connecticut Avenue, the otherwise unexceptional **Nanny O'Brien's** owns the distinction of being the narrowest bar in town and, consequently, the most crowded. Even when nobody's there. (Patrons nonetheless make room for spirited bouts of weekly Irish dancing.) The biggest of them all, the **Dubliner,** may have four rooms, two bars, and its own signature microbrew, but, according to Irish author Tim Pat Coogan in the *Washington Post*, it's still not the real thing: "Not enough smell of urine." Within sight of the Capitol, the Dubliner attracts an older Hill crowd; in contrast, the adjacent **Kelly's Irish Times** is a favorite with Catholic University kids, even though C.U.A. is way up in Northeast. Set in a pagoda-style building with a leprechaun lawn ornament perched on the roof, the small, cozy Irish Times tends to its national icons: Until recently it was the site of an annual 35-hour marathon reading of James Joyce's *Ulysses.*

Murphy's, tucked behind the Woodley Park Metro, preserves its unhurried neighborhood feel by being blessedly hard to find. The standing-room-only Murphy's branch in Alexandria offers a much-needed respite from the colonial and nautical themes that dominate King Street. **Ireland's Own,** also in Alexandria, commemorates visits by Ronald Reagan and George Bush in its foyer and features mediocre menu selections with contrived names like "Tipperary Grilled Cheese" and "Belfast Buffalo Wings." This place has all the ambience of a hotel lounge, tucked as it is behind a row of storefronts, prominent among which is an Irish import shop. Your grandmother could knock back a Guinness here without feeling out of place.

Where the jocks hang out... Sure, you can watch television sports in your own home—but maybe not on 32-inch TVs. Washington's most popular sports bar, **Champions,** is incongruously set in a prim-looking, white three-story house at the end of a narrow alleyway in Georgetown. Its decorating scheme is equal parts sports memorabilia and drunken jock, and its claim to preeminence derives from frequent visits by players on Washington's professional sports teams. **The Rock,** handily located down the block from the District's new MCI Arena, feels less like a crowded locker room, though it's still charged with testosterone. A black-and-white photograph of a hockey player's pulverized face on the second-floor landing provides ample incentive to remain a spectator.

Fanatics Sports Bar and Grill—"Six satellites! 28 TVs!"—is the Dr. Jekyll persona of Archibald's (see The Club Scene), the strip club with which it shares a foundation. Washington's Latino soccer fans crowd into **Guapo's** in Tenleytown to watch their national teams from Central and South America and their country's stars who play on teams in the U.S. The decor is festive, there's a patio out front, and everyone's welcome, even those who can't name the goalie for Bolivia's national team. It used to be said that the sun never sets on the British Empire; that still seems true at **Summers,** a sprawling bar and restaurant in Arlington where every table is bathed in the televised glow of an English Premier League Soccer match. There's nothing like quaffing a Guinness and watching the FA Cup final live from England—at 8am.

Dupont haunts... Dupont Circle's **Brickskeller** boasts over 600 different kinds of beer and what it claims is the nation's largest display of antique (empty) beer cans. Watch out, the exotic imports can be pricey. **Mr. Eagan's** is a comfortably scruffy Dupont Circle fixture with a caricature of its bewhiskered owner painted on the front window; Mr. Eagan himself often stands beside himself to watch the passing pedestrians' double-takes. Locals come for the pubby atmosphere and the unpretentious vibe. And then there's **Timberlake's,** another pleasantly gimmickless Dupont Circle bar which serves as a reminder that the term "ordinary" isn't necessarily pejorative. What it's got is sometimes all you want: friendly faces, a big old jukebox, cheap beer. The same can be said of the more raucous **The Fox and Hounds,** a favorite of the post-college, pre-enough-money-to-go-somewhere-nice crowd.

The singles scene... Leaving aside the beery college-age scene in Georgetown, where can the unattached find a match with a compatible party affiliation and GS rating? An older crowd gathers after work at the **Capitol City Brewing Company** downtown. This is lust with a briefcase; during peak hours there's time to conduct an entire courtship while waiting in line. The movies in the main room at Arlington's **Bardo Rodeo,** which teems with scene-makers in their 20s and 30s, provide serviceable jumping-off points for chatting up strangers (wrong approach: "You like Steven Seagall? I like Steven Seagall!"); they're played at such high volume that it's a boon for dull conversationalists. Though its print ads feature mounted riders chasing down charging elephants, **The Big Hunt** is not about big game—not exactly, anyway. The name proudly proclaims this Dupont Circle bar's identity as a 20-something singles mart, as does its slogan: "Happy hunting ground for humans in the pursuit of mates." With pressure like this, it's a good thing there are 27 brews on tap.

Men to men... Washingtonians, as a tribe, feel safest in the middle of the road; a respected gay Congressman like Barney Frank is one thing, but "out" doesn't equal "outrageous" in D.C. The District is not for the homophobic—it's not at all unusual to see same-sex couples holding hands—but the sleazy side of District gay life maintains a low profile; to find it check out the ads in the back of the *Washington Blade* or in the *Metro Weekly* (both available at Lambda Rising in Dupont Circle, 1525 Connecticut Avenue, NW). Gays do play a disproportionately large role in D.C. nightlife—after all, somebody has to party, and the breeders sure aren't doing it. Among the mainstream choices, **Mr. P's,** Dupont Circle's oldest gay bar, has a happy "hour" that lasts from 3 to 9pm. Now *that's* happy. This easygoing bar and club has room to dance as well as a popular outdoor patio.

At **JR's** (definitely not to be confused with JP's, the upper Georgetown strip joint), exposed brick, varnished wood, and stained glass provide the backdrop for events like "Melrose Mondays," when TV watchers get drink specials whenever Doug Savant, who plays the show's gay character, appears on screen. Along the front facade of **The Fireplace**, what appear to be opaque glass panels featuring a crackling log fire are actually made of one-way glass through which passersby are visible to patrons inside. Know this before you stop near the window to adjust your tie (or lipstick, or nose ring, or whatever). For a completely different take on the gay scene, try **Remington's** on Capitol Hill, which offers line-dancing lessons during the week and chances to show off your new skill on Sundays (appropriate Western dress expected). Remington's caters to an older gay crowd. Proof? They also have bingo. Lesbians should check out Phase One and Hung Jury (see The Club Scene).

For the martini set... Ozio owner George Christacos once called D.C. "the worst large city in the world for nightlife"; if so, he's certainly not to blame. This "martini and cigar lounge" is the flagship for D.C.'s burgeoning cigar revolution. Its menus proclaim one of Winston Churchill's Rules of Life: "Smoking cigars and drinking of alcohol before, after, and if need be, during all meals, and intervals between them." A vast underground cavern with wide columns and art deco–style couches, Ozio has a certain subterranean elegance. It also has an underwhelming and overpriced tapas menu, but its chief attractions are infinite variations on the common martini (at $6 a glass, maybe not so common after all) and glass-walled walk-in humidor. Martinis and stogies are also the leitmotif at **Felix** (see The Club Scene), which hosts a "Cigar & Martini Party" on Saturdays and whose "Sinatra Wednesdays" feature the jazz trio Martini Red—and martinis and cigars, of course. On warm nights the doors to Felix's big front room are opened to let cool jazz and floor-length purple curtains billow out onto the sidewalk. Upstairs at **Red Sage** (see Late Night Dining), under a sky-blue ceiling streaked with painted-on cirrus clouds, sophisticates still gather late to share single-malt scotch or a bottle of wine from the extensive wine list, which includes the restaurant's own vintage.

For beer nuts... There was a time when the only question they asked about your beer order was "can or bottle?" The brand was bound to be Miller or Schlitz or Pabst, because there just wasn't much else. Things are more complicated these days. At Dupont Circle's **Brickskeller,** where you can get hundreds of beers you never heard of from countries you never knew existed, the bar staff will open cans from the bottom to preserve them as collectibles. Also in the Dupont Circle area, the ongoing kegger that is **The Big Hunt** has 27 beers on tap—including many locals brewed in Maryland and Virginia. Georgetown jazz bar **The Saloun** has 18 beers on tap and 52 more in bottles. Arlington's **Galaxy Hut,** a small place with a big beer menu, rates the astonishing superlative of having the best beer selection on Wilson Boulevard, with 14 on tap and three dozen in bottles.

Do-it-themselves beer... Designer beer is as ubiquitous in Washington as it is everywhere else. Arlington's **Bardo Rodeo** is the area's foremost purveyor of such—indeed, it claims to be the biggest brewpub in the western hemisphere. But the coziness implied in the term "brewpub" just doesn't apply here. A totem pole stands out front, crowned with the single word "Beer" in pointy letters. The place occupies the premises of an old car dealership: A late-sixties Plymouth Fury III protrudes through the bar's front window. Patrons sit at wobbly tables on white plastic patio chairs in the bar's largest room, where a cinema-scale movie screen shows movies you don't want to see (usually starring Chuck Norris) with the volume up so loud you can't talk. So devoted is Bardo to the dissemination of everybody's favorite malt beverage that they actually *deliver* beer (call 703/527–2121). Ads for this uncommon service smirk, "Remember the milk man?"

There is a slightly—okay, entirely—different ambiance at the **Capitol City Brewing Company,** a splashy downtown brewpub in what was once a Greyhound station. The happy hour site of choice among the young and the suit-wearing, Capitol City has soaring ceilings, a huge circular bar, and a menu featuring real food. The first business since the fall of Prohibition licensed to brew alcohol in the District, Cap City has an ever-increasing number of locations; there are now offshoots near Union Station and in Arlington. If your interest in beer is stronger than your interest in flower-bearing trees, Cap City makes an aromatic microbrew called "Cherry Blossom Ale"—25 pounds of cherries are used in each batch of this fruity (and we mean that as a compliment) beer. Alexandria's **Virginia Beverage Company** offers a slight variation on the brewpub theme: Its decor is Ethan Allen where Capital City's is postindustrial. There are shiny copper vats in the front windows, a pressed-tin ceiling, polished cherry booths, and microbrewed sodas on the menu for teetotalers, but beware: It's the kind of place that carries a line of merchandise bearing its logo.

Want to concoct a brew of your own? **Shenandoah Brewing Company,** a sociable establishment in west Alexandria, will sell you all the ingredients, let you loose on their clean new equipment, and walk you through the process of brewing any of 12 styles of beer. It takes about 3 hours and costs from $85 to $120 (plus $30 for bottles) per 15-gallon batch, around $5 a six-pack, but you have to wait a month until you can drink the stuff.

House drinks... Several D.C. destinations serve not-to-be-missed specialty drinks. U Street's trendy **Chi-Cha Lounge** features red and white "chi-cha," a Latin American punch that its menu claims enabled the ancient Incas to comprehend the mysteries of the universe. The thick liquid comes in small glasses and has a rich fruit-and-nut flavor reminiscent of banana bread. (To be fair, it tastes better than it sounds.) As its subtitle implies, **Ozio,** a downtown "martini and cigar lounge," specializes in martinis. Here, the simple *Webster's* definition—a cocktail made of gin and dry vermouth—is left far behind; all that Ozio's constantly changing exotic array have in common is the classic martini glass. At the **9:30** rock club near U Street (see The Club Scene), the house specialty is the "blue thing," a mix of vodka, blue curacao, and the pulverized ice we all know from Slurpees. Come to think of it, what blue things most resemble is a Slurpee with a little more kick. You can ask for a "swirlie" without fear at the **Austin Grill** in upper Georgetown (see Late Night Dining), which serves a combination strawberry and lime margarita entwined in a single glass. The drink takes its moniker from the fraternity prank of the same name—something involving holding a guy's head in a flushing toilet—but don't hold that against it. In keeping with its Russian theme, U Street's **State of the Union** (see The Club Scene) features a formidable collection of flavored vodkas. These range from watermelon to ginger, but don't let the candy-counter-sounding names fool you—this stuff will knock you to your knees. And at Georgetown's **Music City Roadhouse** (see Late Night Dining), a summertime favorite is the pitchers of lemonade spiked with schnapps, liqueur, you name it.

Neighborhood hangouts... The popularity of some places is inexplicable to outsiders, which usually suits the regulars just fine. In Cleveland Park, this certainly applies to the **Oxford Tavern,** better known as the **Zoo Bar**—the blue, purple, and green neon sign outside even has it in double quotes. There's a wild-animal mural inside this small Connecticut Avenue bar and, on hot nights when the outdoor patio is crowded, you can hear the occasional bray or yelp from the National Zoo directly across the street. In Dupont Circle, the corresponding neighborhood stalwart is **The Fox and Hounds,** whose English-countryside-evoking name is in no way manifested by the bar's ambience or decor. In fact, it's a dark, crowded place with surly waitresses and a whole lotta Led Zeppelin on the jukebox. It was after a visit to the Fox and Hounds that a friend of a friend threw up in my car—which, in its own way, is an altogether appropriate testimonial to the place.

To call a place a neighborhood hangout is to imply that it has a loyal clientele but no obvious attributes; judging by the extent to which it meets both these criteria, **Dan's** in Adams-Morgan is the quintessential neighborhood hangout. On Capitol Hill, **Tune Inn** has taken having no good points to new heights by actually becoming famous for it. No doubt it helps that the neighborhood hangers-out happen to be such movers and shakers.

One Hill of a good time... As a group, the bars on Capitol Hill are the kind you go to because they're nearby—you'd never, say, drive from Dupont Circle to a Hill bar. But given that folks who work on the Hill can spare so little of their busy lives for partying, a few bars will always thrive here. Though 1600 Pennsylvania Avenue (NW) gets all the press, the 300 block of Pennsylvania (SE) is where the action is—at the **Tune Inn,** for instance, that most famous of Capitol Hill bars. Universally derided (or praised) as charmless—you need look no further than the dead plants in the front window—this bar has been a Hillie hangout for more than 40 years. (Such are its highfalutin associations that *Esquire* magazine once named it one of the 100 best bars in America.) The decor runs to dead animals; in fact, officials from the U.S. Fish and Wildlife Service have identified no fewer than five endangered species among its stuffed birds (this type of scrutiny is the downside to a Capitol Hill location).

The Tune Inn is where James Carville and Mary Matalin went on their first date; like most people, she insisted on leaving and going next door to the **Hawk and Dove.** Opened in 1967, the Hawk and Dove got its name in the days when its regulars were divided into those who violently opposed and those who ardently supported the Vietnam War. Local legend has it that the factions drew a dividing line on the floor. It's still crowded with Hillies young and old, but the atmosphere is slightly less strained—today's political issues (the balanced budget, for instance) just don't generate lines on the floor. Under the same management is **Jenkins Hill** (the title comes from Capitol Hill's original name), which was reportedly a favorite of Richard Nixon—he liked the stained glass behind the bar. In addition to bearing this distinction, it's also a sports bar, dance club, and—on Fridays and Saturdays—a 24-hour restaurant. This place attracts the Capitol's workaday spillover as well as young locals, especially on weekends when, Hill-wise, its late-night food is the only game in town. **Bullfeathers** takes its name from Teddy Roosevelt's famed euphemistic interjection, and its turn-of-the-century ambience from the era of his presidency. An older Hill contingent congregates here to speak softly but order a big drink.

Pub crawl, Georgetown style... Tourist-heavy Georgetown's one unique bar, the late Marquis de Rochambeau—resplendent in dirty plastic flowers and old velvet—has shuttered. Nevertheless, if expectations are diminished, several Georgetown bars offer respite for the weary and thirsty. Close to the Georgetown University campus is **The Tombs,** Bill Clinton's college hangout and the model for the bar in the 1985 Brat Pack film *St. Elmo's Fire.* The bar, hung with oars from Georgetown's winning crew teams, has a vaguely turn-of-the-century air—or would if somebody would turn down the Stone Temple Pilots. **The Saloun** has live jazz and blues every night as well as 75 different kinds of beer. When packed with revelers, it looks and sounds like an indoor Mardi Gras. Spacious **Garrett's,** with two floors, three bars, and an outdoor patio, is distinguished by the mounted rhino glowering in the downstairs bar, no doubt checking out frat boys and their putative dates. Nearby **Winston's** was supposedly so popular with Gerald Ford's daughter, Susan, that she was awarded a personalized bar stool. These days, she'd have to push a half-dozen pre-law students in stonewashed jeans out of her way to find somewhere to sit. Another collegiate hangout, **Charing Cross,** suffers from some thematic confusion: It's named after a London train station, yet decorated with photographs of Marilyn Monroe. **Mr. Smith's,** its front windows plastered with flyers complaining about its omission from *Washingtonian* magazine's "Best of" list, calls itself "the friendliest bar in town" (friendly, but assertive). College types congregate here for protracted outdoor beer-nursing and other unmolested dawdling. Venerable **Nathan's,** which presides over Georgetown's Wisconsin Avenue and M Street hub, is the cloth-napkin alternative to the collegiate watering holes, hung with tasteful nautical and sporting prints—not the place to start a tankard-waving sing-along.

Old Town taverns... Out in Old Town Alexandria, King Street's brick-and-brass circuit begins with the **Seaport Inn.** Nestled on the bank of the Potomac, the building has a suitable patina of history—it was purchased in 1778 by John Fitzgerald, George Washington's military aide-de-camp, and legend has it that the pair quaffed many an ale on the premises. (These days, they'd be at the Mayflower Hotel's Town & Country Lounge with all the other political bigwigs.) Mere steps away, hordes of drinkers pack the bright streetside windows of **Union**

Street, a two-story brick "Public House" (yet another euphemism for "bar") with the requisite exposed beams and vintage decor. Union Street functions as a sort of TGIFriday's for the laptop-and-cell-phone set. Back on King Street and up a flight of stairs, the **Basin Street Lounge** is a jazz venue that, with its floral carpeting, red velvet curtains, and equestrian prints, could pass for an antebellum dining room. If you find the atmosphere stifling, pop downstairs to the **Bayou Room** for a beer amid taxidermied wall hangings and considerably more animated yuppie partiers. Farther still up King Street is **King Pepper,** part bar, part dance club. Its attempt to provide Alexandria with a funky Adams-Morgan-style nightspot is commendable but unsuccessful; the music here is more likely to be top 40 than techno. Despite the wacky playing-cards-and-peppers motif, it's a fern bar at heart. **Ireland's Own** and **Murphy's** cater to Alexandria's Guinness set, geriatric and Gen X, respectively.

How to wake the dead in Arlington... If you skip over to Arlington and cruise Wilson Boulevard, look for **Whitlow's on Wilson,** a bar and restaurant that moved here from its original location at the corner of 11th and E streets in D.C. Its rec-room-with-waitresses atmosphere feels comfortable as an old pair of jeans: Its three connected rooms include everything from foosball tables to diner-style booths, as well as eccentric touches like a nonworking jukebox with a menu of unplayable selections like the Captain and Tennille's "Muskrat Love." Upping the hipness ante (if not comfort level), is nearby **Galaxy Hut,** a small bar with a menu of exotic beers, walls hung with local art, and year-round garlands of Christmas-tree lights. Though it's been known to host poetry readings, Galaxy Hut's main attractions are performances by local bands who push the tables aside and squeeze in up front. It's a tight fit: Amps get unplugged midset when someone steps on the cord. Across the street, newly expanded **Iota** (see The Club Scene) has a more ample performance space for locals and attracts a somewhat older crowd—the 30-something and the 30-something-at-heart. Megabar **Bardo Rodeo,** with its blaring movies and car-crash decor, is Wilson Boulevard's headline act. The area's newest nightspot, apparently intent on replicating the scale and success of Bardo Rodeo, is nearby **Clarendon**

Grill. Inside is a big, open room with high ceilings and gallery lighting and a long bar made of stacked oil drums; outside is a large patio area. Some aspects of the decor are a bit strained—for instance, the huge paintings of cereal boxes on the walls. But it may prove a respite from what can become a mob scene at Bardo.

Making the Adams-Morgan scene... In the late 1970s, when Adams-Morgan was a daring new nightlife destination, the building on Columbia Road that now houses **Perry's** was home to a club called Morgan's, which regulars recall as being the closest Washington has ever come to a high-flying Studio 54–style nightclub. Perry's is more subdued, though it did spark a local mini-trend a few years ago by instituting a popular drag brunch. The bar and restaurant has the best roof deck in town for dining and drinking. *Do* snag one of the comfy couches; *don't* order the sushi. You can tell which other area bars pre-date the onslaught of hipness by their names. **Millie & Al's,** for instance, is a longtime neighborhood bar, as is **Dan's;** both are as unfashionable—and, by the same token, as unpretentious—as their names suggest. Millie & Al's looks somewhat unremarkable from the outside—and from the inside as well, for that matter. Here you're more likely to find scuffed vinyl than burnished steel. Dan's, with its windowless wooden exterior in shades of blue, looks more like an inexpertly erected clubhouse than a gathering place for grown-ups. The newer drinking establishments, however, have names and gimmicks like the **Toledo Lounge,** a yuppie magnet ineffectually disguised as a 1950s gas station. Perchance you've seen this vintage-Coke-sign-centric decor before.

Tickling the ivories... The piano bar may be regarded by many as an anachronism, but if anyone can prove otherwise, it's local keyboard idol Burnett Thompson. He's not the sort of pianist who wears a powder-blue tuxedo and sets a giant brandy snifter on the baby grand for tips. Rather, Thompson is a classical pianist who plays at the **West End Cafe** in the Washington Circle Hotel when he's not performing with one of the many area orchestral ensembles with which he's affiliated. If you hate the colorless piano-bar repertoire, walk in and request some Schumann. The hotel itself is lavishly appointed, with a grand circular lobby. The piano bar's habitues—the sort of drinkers whose version of leisurewear is to put on an older tie—are likely to be guests of the hotel or local regulars.

Biker bars... A biker bar in Washington? Well, sort of. **The Crow Bar** has Harleys parked outside and stocks *Motorcycle Times,* but it's also in the heart of downtown D.C., which means weekday patrons are more likely to have laptops than tattoos. Punsterism runs amok in the garish mural on the side of the building—it features a surly looking crow brandishing the eponymous automotive tool.

Big-screen bars... Cinema be damned—what film doesn't drag after you've eaten your last Junior Mint? Two local movie house–cafes have taken the concept of the concession stand to a whole new level—and we *don't* mean those plastic trays of Cheez-Whiz nachos they hawk at Cineplex Odeon. We mean beer. The **Bethesda Theater Cafe,** which shows recently released movies, features a basic hot-dog-and-hamburger menu and draft beer. The popcorn is too salty, but there's no bar top for the customary bowls of thirst-inducing peanuts and pretzels. The scene is the same at the **Arlington Cinema and Draft House,** which features the added benefit of love seats where only couples may sit on Mondays, Fridays, and Saturdays.

Cozying up... Put off by standing ankle-deep in Pabst Blue Ribbon and shouting at your date above the techno-funk? Try the cozy drinking room at the ultracivilized **Tabard Inn,** a Dupont Circle restaurant and hotel as quaint as you'd expect in a hotel whose name comes from *The Canterbury Tales.* It has a crackling fireplace, musty old couches, and overstuffed chairs in a room filled with charmingly crooked gilt-framed landscapes and the quiet hum of conversation. The comfortable seating at the **Chi-Cha Lounge** is conducive to snuggling, as are the low lighting and coffee-table-level votives. The menu instructs patrons to remove their ties. This U Street bar in an old firehouse is distinguished by its defiantly square music—during one recent visit, Barbra Streisand's recording of "People"—and its creative tapas (not to be confused with conventional bar food). On slow nights, they bring out large hookahs, and customers can smoke exotic tobacco in the manner preferred by the caterpillar in *Alice in Wonderland.* For true romance, share a mouthpiece.

The Bar Scene: Index

Note: If no Metro stop is listed, a bar is best reached by taxi or car. The nearest Metro stop to Georgetown is Foggy Botton–GWU, a 15-minute walk or short cab ride away. In Old Town, King Street bars are a straight shot down the street from the King Street Metro stop, but the distance may be as far as 12 blocks.

Arlington Cinema and Draft House. Second-run movies and ballpark food; they go together like...like Mel Gibson and Danny Glover.... *Tel 703/486–2345. 2903 Columbia Pike, Arlington, VA.* **(see pp. 59, 71)**

Bardo Rodeo. Sprawling bar in a onetime car dealership serves its own microbrews.... *Tel 703/527–9399. 2000 Wilson Blvd., Arlington, VA. Clarendon Metro.* **(see pp. 60, 62, 64, 69)**

Basin Street Lounge/Bayou Room. A polite, upscale jazz venue in a faux–Old World setting and a lively basement-level bar, respectively.... *Tel 703/549–1141. 219 King St., Alexandria, VA.* **(see p. 69)**

Bayou Room. See Basin Street Lounge.

Bethesda Theater Cafe. When a box of Milk Duds is not enough.... *Tel 301/656–3337. 7719 Wisconsin Ave., Bethesda, MD. Bethesda Metro.* **(see pp. 59, 71)**

The Big Hunt. The Washington bar scene's self-conscious take on the classic pickup bar.... *Tel 202/785–2333. 1345 Connecticut Ave., NW. Dupont Circle Metro.* **(see pp. 62, 64)**

Brickskeller. A beer connoisseur's dream come true: Pick a latitude and drink your way around the world.... *Tel*

202/293–1885. 1523 22nd St., NW. Dupont Circle Metro. **(see pp. 61, 64)**

Bullfeathers. Clientele at this Hill bar runs the gamut from congressman to intern.... *Tel 202/543–5005. 401 S. 1st St., SE. Capitol South Metro.* **(see pp. 58, 67)**

Capitol City Brewing Company. This bright, shiny showplace of a microbrewery is a happy-hour favorite.... *Tel 202/628–2222, 1100 New York Ave., NW, closes 11pm Sun–Thur, midnight Fri–Sat, Metro Center. Tel 202/842–2337, 2 Massachusetts Ave., NW, Union Station Metro. Tel 703/578–3888, 2700 S. Quincy St., Arlington, VA.* **(see pp. 62, 64)**

Champions. Stomping ground for 20-something guys in baseball caps.... *Tel 202/965–4005. 1206 Wisconsin Ave., NW.* **(see p. 61)**

Charing Cross. The name may sound Anglophilic, but this collegiate watering hole is quintessential Georgetown.... *Tel 202/388–21412. 3027 M St., NW.* **(see p. 68)**

Chi-Cha Lounge. It's not a furniture showroom, it just looks like one. Choose a couch to fit your mood and settle in for the evening.... *Tel 202/234–8400. 1624 U St., NW. U Street–Cardozo Metro.* **(see pp. 59, 65, 71)**

Clarendon Grill. Gallerylike Arlington watering hole.... *Tel 703/524–7455. 1101 N. Highland St., Arlington, VA. Clarendon Metro.* **(see p. 69)**

The Crow Bar. Despite the biker trappings, this downtown bar near the K Street business artery is strictly middle-of-the-road.... *Tel 202/223–2972. 1006 20th St., NW. Farragut North Metro.* **(see pp. 60, 71)**

Dan's. Nondescript Adams-Morgan bar that elicits fanatical loyalty from locals.... *Tel 202/265–9241. 2315 18th St., NW. Woodley Park–Zoo Metro.* **(see pp. 66, 70)**

Dave & Buster's. Video—and more, much more—arcade for grown-ups.... *Tel 301/230–5151. White Flint Mall, 11301 Rockville Pike, North Bethesda, MD. White Flint Metro.* **(see p. 59)**

Doubletree Hotel. Across the Potomac, with a spectacular nighttime view of Washington.... *Tel 703/416–4100. 300 Army-Navy Dr., Crystal City, VA. Crystal City Metro.* **(see p. 59)**

Dubliner. Capitol Hill Irish bar.... *Tel 202/737–3773. 520 N. Capitol St., NW. Union Station Metro.* **(see pp. 58, 60)**

Fanatics Sports Bar and Grill. Lively downtown sports bar shares space with a strip joint. Not the best place to meet women.... *Tel 202/737–7678. 1520 K St., NW. Farragut North Metro.* **(see p. 61)**

The Fireplace. Deceptively sedate-looking Dupont Circle gay bar.... *Tel 202/293–1293. 2161 P St., NW. Dupont Circle Metro.* **(see p. 63)**

The Fox and Hounds. Classic, friendly dive with heavy metal on the jukebox and an outdoor patio that overflows in summertime.... *Tel 202/232–6307. 1537 17th St., NW. Dupont Circle Metro.* **(see pp. 62, 66)**

Galaxy Hut. Small Arlington hole-in-the-wall for alterna-kids.... *Tel 703/525–8646. 2711 Wilson Blvd., Arlington, VA. Clarendon Metro.* **(see pp. 64, 69)**

Garrett's. The largest of the homogeneous frat-boy bars on Georgetown's M Street drinking circuit.... *Tel 202/333–1033. 3003 M St., NW.* **(see p. 68)**

Guapo's. Mexican eatery doubles as a small-screen soccer stadium in upper Northwest.... *Tel 202/686–3588. 4515 Wisconsin Ave., NW. Tenleytown–AU Metro.* **(see p. 61)**

Hawk and Dove. Most historic of the Capitol Hill bars; a repository of political anecdotes.... *Tel 202/543–3300. 329 Pennsylvania Ave., SE. Capitol South Metro.* **(see p. 58, 67)**

Ireland's Four Provinces. Homey Irish bar where even the toilet stalls are green.... *Tel 202/244–0860. 3412 Connecticut Ave., NW. Cleveland Park Metro.* **(see p. 60)**

Ireland's Own. Tourist-oriented Irish bar in Old Town.... *Tel 703/549–4535. 132 N. Royal St., Alexandria, VA. King Street Metro.* **(see pp. 60, 69)**

Jenkins Hill. Comfortable neighborhood restaurant and bar in the neighborhood of the Capitol.... *Tel 202/544–4066. 319 Pennsylvania Ave., SE. Capitol South Metro.* **(see p. 67)**

JR's. Cavernous 17th Street gay bar known for its nighttime scenester vibe and the hilarity of its TV parties.... *Tel 202/328–0090. 1519 17th St., NW. Dupont Circle Metro.* **(see p. 63)**

Kelly's Irish Times. Impossibly cozy Irish bar across from Union Station.... *Tel 202/543–5433. 14 F St., NW. Union Station Metro.* **(see pp. 58, 60)**

King Pepper. Likable if somewhat featureless Old Town restaurant/bar/club.... *Tel 703/299–9153. 808 King St., Alexandria, VA.* **(see p. 69)**

Mayflower Hotel. Comes by its nickname—"the grande dame of Washington hotels"—honestly.... *Tel 202/347–3000. 1127 Connecticut Ave., NW. Farragut North Metro.* **(see p. 58)**

Millie & Al's. Veteran Adams-Morgan watering hole.... *Tel 202/387–8131. 2440 18th St., NW. Woodley Park–Zoo Metro.* **(see p. 70)**

Mr. Eagan's. Longtime Dupont Circle bar that pre-dates the martini-and-acid-jazz movement by a good decade.... *Tel 202/861–9609. 1343 Connecticut Ave., NW. Dupont Circle Metro.* **(see p. 61)**

Mr. P's. Reputed to be the oldest gay bar in Dupont Circle (but don't bother looking for the plaque from the National Register of Historic Places).... *Tel 202/293–1064. 2147 P St., NW. Dupont Circle Metro.* **(see p. 63)**

Mr. Smith's. Casual collegiate eatery in Georgetown.... *Tel 202/333–3104. 3104 M St., NW.* **(see p. 68)**

Murphy's. Call it a law: There's no such thing as too many Irish bars.... *Tel 202/462–7171, 2605 24th St., NW, Woodley Park–Zoo Metro. Tel 703/548–1717, 713 King St., Alexandria, VA.* **(see pp. 60, 69)**

Nanny O'Brien's. Neighborhood Irish bar that keeps Emerald Isle trappings to a minimum.... *Tel 202/686–9189. 3319 Connecticut Ave., NW. Cleveland Park Metro.* **(see p. 60)**

Nathan's. Relatively restrained corner Georgetown bar and restaurant.... *Tel 202/338–2600. 3150 M St., NW.* **(see p. 68)**

Oxford Tavern. See Zoo Bar.

Ozio. A cave-like bastion of cigar smoking, martini guzzling, and cosmopolitan posturing.... *Tel 202/822–6000. 1835 K St., NW. Farragut North Metro. Closed Sun.* **(see pp. 59, 63, 65)**

Perry's. Urbane Adams-Morgan bar and restaurant.... *Tel 202/234–6218. 1811 Columbia Rd., NW. Woodley Park–Zoo Metro.* **(see pp. 59, 70)**

Remington's An anomaly in more ways than one—a gay country-and-western bar on Capitol Hill.... *Tel 202/543–3113. 639 Pennsylvania Ave., SE. Eastern Market Metro.* **(see p. 63)**

The Rock. Brand-spanking-new multilevel sports bar within sight of the city's brand-spanking-new downtown sports arena.... *Tel 202/842–7625. 717 6th St., NW. Gallery Place–Chinatown Metro.* **(see p. 61)**

The Saloun. Nightly live music by local jazz and blues artists in this Georgetown bistro.... *Tel 202/965–4900. 3239 M St., NW.* **(see pp. 64, 68)**

Seaport Inn. An outrageously historic Alexandria bar—really puts the "old" in Old Town.... *Tel 703/549–2341. 6 King St., Alexandria, VA. King Street Metro.* **(see p. 68)**

Shenandoah Brewing Company. Sociable brew-it-yourself establishment for novice away-from-home brewers.... *Tel 703/823–9508. 652 Pickett St., Alexandria, VA. Van Dorn Metro.* **(see p. 65)**

Summers. Inconspicuous Arlington bar and restaurant where fans of British soccer gather.... *Tel 703/528–8278. 1520 N. Courthouse Rd., Arlington, VA. Court House Metro.* **(see p. 61)**

Tabard Inn. Perhaps the city's nicest place to sit and sip.... *Tel 202/833–2668. 1739 N St., NW. Dupont Circle Metro. Closes daily at midnight.* **(see p. 71)**

Timberlake's. Neighborhood hangout with what may well be the friendliest bartenders in town.... *Tel 202/483–2266. 1726 Connecticut Ave., NW. Dupont Circle Metro.* **(see p. 62)**

Toledo Lounge. Yuppie enclave in Adams-Morgan.... *Tel 202/986–5416. 2435 18th St., NW. Woodley Park-Zoo Metro.* **(see p. 70)**

The Tombs. You'll look conspicuous without your calculus homework at this Georgetown University near-campus hangout.... *Tel 202/337–6668. 1226 36th St., NW.* **(see p. 68)**

Tune Inn. Notoriously unprepossessing and enduringly popular Capital Hill slumming spot.... *Tel 202/543–2725. 331 ½ Pennsylvania Ave., SE. Capitol South Metro.* **(see pp. 66, 67)**

Union Street. Rambling five-room bar and restaurant in Old Town Alexandria.... *Tel 703/548–1785. 121 S. Union St., Alexandria, VA. King Street Metro.* **(see p. 68)**

Virginia Beverage Company. Modern suburban microbrewery.... *Tel 703/684–5397. 607 King St., Alexandria, VA.* **(see p. 65)**

West End Cafe The city's least stereotypical piano bar.... *Tel 202/293–5390. Washington Circle Hotel, 1 Washington Circle. Foggy Bottom–GWU Metro.* **(see p. 70)**

Whitlow's on Wilson. Roomy Arlington bar and restaurant with a low-key Formica-and-linoleum ambiance.... *Tel 703/276–9693. 2854 Wilson Blvd., Arlington, VA. Clarendon Metro.* **(see p. 69)**

Willard Inter-Continental Hotel. The most historic hotel in a city that's lousy with 'em.... *Tel 202/628–9100. 1401 Pennsylvania Ave., NW. Metro Center.* **(see p. 58)**

Winston's. The music is loud, the line long, the patrons rambunctious 20-somethings.... *Tel 202/333-3150. 3295 M St., NW.* **(see p. 68)**

Zoo Bar. Twenty-somethings from Connecticut Avenue apartments pack this remarkably unremarkable neighborhood hangout, officially named the Oxford Tavern.... *Tel 202/232–4225. 3000 Connecticut Ave., NW. Woodley Park-Zoo Metro.* **(see p. 66)**

the

3
arts

If you still imagine Washington as a cultural backwater, maybe you've spent too much time watching reactionary members of Congress fulminate against the arts on TV. The truth is that the Jesses and Newts are speaking for their own constituencies—certainly not for Washingtonians, whose high level of affluence, education, and yuppie sensibility demands a full complement of culturally redeeming pastimes. Okay, so there used to be a time when D.C. couldn't tell its Brecht from its Bach. But that era ended on September 8, 1971, when the John F. Kennedy Center for the Performing Arts celebrated its grand opening with the world premiere of Leonard Bernstein's *Requiem Mass* honoring President Kennedy. With this event, Washington began its metamorphosis from cultural Nowheresville to world-class center of the performing arts. Just downriver from the Watergate, the six-theater complex attracts audiences for the National Symphony Orchestra (NSO) and Washington Opera, Broadway road shows and Important Theatrical Events, ballet, modern dance, folk music, jazz, and cinema. And now that its Concert Hall has been rendered acoustically correct—to the tune of $50 million—NSO director Leonard Slatkin has vowed to make his ensemble "The National Symphony Orchestra—of the United States of America."

Not unexpectedly in a town whose major natural resource is words, Washington's strongest arts sector is the theater. That began happening back in 1950 with the opening of Arena Stage, one of America's pioneer regional theater companies. Today, the Washington area also supports some 30 professional theater companies and stages, plus countless non-Equity troupes. Big-ticket pre- and post-Broadway runs that don't play Kennedy Center usually sojourn at the Warner Theater or The National Theatre, two restored gems in downtown D.C.'s wannabe Theater District.

Of course, there are still some artistic areas that need improvement. The NSO's great expectations notwithstanding, Washington's classical music scene better befits a city of under 600,000 people (which it is) than the capital of a nation of 265 million (which it also is). Beyond Kennedy Center and DAR Constitution Hall, you probably have to hie yourself to a college, museum, or house of worship to hear serious music. The dance scene remains minimal, a step or two behind the curve. While the District has held onto its performing-arts institutions pretty firmly (far better than it has retained retail outlets, for example), the suburbs are making impressive inroads. Several hinterland theaters—notably Signature Theatre Company in Virginia and the Olney Theatre and Round House Theatre in Maryland—adamantly refuse to make "suburban" synonymous with "lightweight." And with its voluminous schedule of class acts in all areas of the performing arts, George Mason University's Center for the Arts in Fairfax, Virginia, could be (but definitely is not) called Kennedy Off-Center.

Sources

On Fridays, the ***Washington Post*** Weekend supplement lists every concert, recital, dance, play, and other performance around the region for the entire week. On other days, the *Post*'s "Guide to the Lively Arts" has succinct listings for that day only. D.C.'s other daily newspaper, the Moonie-owned ***Washington Times,*** includes quite thorough listings for the week ahead in its Washington Weekend section, which comes out on Thursday, thus getting a one-day jump on the *Post.* Listings in the free weekly ***Washington City Paper,*** with separate headings for music, theater, dance, comedy, events, exhibits, and performance art, are most comprehensive of all. Stacks of the *Washington City Paper* begin materializing after noon on Thursday in sidewalk boxes, bookstores, music stores, libraries, and office buildings all over the Washington area, but by the weekend they've vanished—that's how useful those listings are.

Several online services keep minute track of the performing-arts scene, which can be handy for hooked-up out-of-towners who can't get the local papers but want to scope out the territory in advance. Both the ***Washington Post*** (http://washingtonpost.com) and ***Washington City Paper*** (http://www.washingtoncitypaper.com) virtually duplicate their arts and entertainment listings. **Washington Sidewalk** (http://www.washington.sidewalk.com), part of Microsoft's Internet network, runs schedules and reviews of local performances. Along with its own reviews, ShireNet's **Area Arts Events** (http://www.shirenet.com) provides hot links to the home pages of local theaters and arenas. **D.C. Yahoo!** (http://www.yahoo.com) links into websites operated by other events listers and the institutions themselves. The website of the local public classical music station, **WETA** (FM 90.9), posts listings of area events and mini-reviews by in-house arts mavens (http://weta.org).

Getting Tickets

Major theaters like Kennedy Center, the Shakespeare Theatre, Warner Theater, and the National Theatre handle their own charge-by-phone ticketing, with box-office pick-up any time before the show. To buy tickets to other venues you'll have to do business with (and pay exorbitant surcharges to) ticket outlets. Two agencies divide all the action: **TicketMaster** (tel 703/432–SEAT, 800/551–7328) and **Protix** (tel 703/638–1908). TicketMaster also sells tickets at Tower Records and Hecht's department stores, but for cash only. Many of the smaller theaters will hold a reservation if you give them a charge-card number, with no surcharges.

The preceding applies to full-price tickets. In Washington you can also pay more or less than list price. On the discount side, **TICKETplace** sells day-of-show tickets to plays, concerts, dance performances, and opera at 60 performing-arts venues in D.C. and the burbs (including Kennedy Center) for half the face value of the ticket, plus a 10-percent service charge. Selection varies, however, and availability is much higher for weeknight performances than for weekends. Occasionally, TICKETplace also offers half-price tickets for performances the next day or even later that week—you might get lucky. To find out what's available, call the TICKETplace information line (tel 202/TICKETS) or hook up on the Web (http://www.cultural-alliance.org/tickets). TICKETplace is located in the northeast corner of the Old Post Office Pavilion (11th Street at Pennsylvania Ave. NW, Federal Triangle Metro); it's open Tuesday through Saturday from 11am to 6pm. Tickets for Sunday and Monday performances, when available, go on sale Saturday. All tickets are sold in person on a first-come basis, for cash or American Express traveler's checks—no credit cards accepted.

On the other end of the spectrum, ticket brokers are available to accommodate those who absolutely positively have to be there—and are willing to pay the price. Ticket brokers are scalpers who somehow (don't ask them how) come up with the best seats in the house and otherwise unavailable tickets to sold-out performances (as well as Redskins and Orioles games). **Top Centre Ticket Service** (tel 202/452–9040, 2000 Pennsylvania Ave., NW) has a counter in the same mall as Tower Records (TicketMaster). The other brokers are all reachable by phone in Maryland: **Encore Tickets** (tel 301/718–2525, 800/296–3626), **The Ticket Connection** (tel 301/587–6850), and **Ticket Finders** (tel 301/927–8000, http://www.ticketfinders.com). Expect to pay an arm and a leg (and maybe a couple of fingers) for tickets—double the face value and up. Call around to various agencies for the best price (competition is fierce). Also check out ads from other ticket brokers in the *Post's* daily "Tickets-Entertainment" classifieds section, where you may also spot ads from a few "real" people trying to unload tickets for realistic prices.

The Lowdown

Theater District?... Yes, Virginia (and Maryland), Washington does have a Theater District—or so the cultural powers-that-be have dubbed the mainstream performance venues scattered on or near Pennsylvania Avenue between 7th and 14th streets, NW. This cluster crests with two elegant spaces on the corner of 13th Street and Pennsylvania Avenue, **The National Theatre** and the **Warner Theater**. A renovated movie and vaudeville house, with gilded balconies in the auditorium and a brewpub in the basement, the Warner Theater specializes in Broadway road shows, concerts, comedy, and big-time magic acts. Since The National Theatre was established in 1835, it has, in various incarnations, showcased everything from John Wilkes Booth and "Swedish Nightingale" Jenny Lind to Tracy and Hepburn; the Arlington brother/sister act of Shirley MacLaine and Warren Beatty were once, respectively, usherette and stage doorman here. Nowadays, hopeful shows en route to Broadway and Broadway hits making their tour of the provinces usually wind up here. Monday Night at the National offers a mixed bag of freebies at 6 and 7:30pm.

Still living down Booth's notorious walk-on during *The American Cousin,* the restored **Ford's Theatre** features family-friendly Americana-themed plays and musicals, plus a cockles-warming production of *A Christmas Carol* every Yuletide, from the week before Thanksgiving to New Year's Eve. On a small stage within D.C.'s oldest Catholic Church, **Washington Stage Guild** specializes in overlooked gems, little-known works by well-known playwrights, and new stuff, performed by top local actors between more remunerative gigs. The resident company of the esteemed **Shakespeare Theatre** often imports a medium-magnitude star (Kelly McGillis, Harry Hamlin,

Stacy Keach) for lead roles in its mostly Shakespeare six-play season.

Off-Pennsylvania Avenue... When it opened in 1950, **Arena Stage**—boldly located south of downtown by Washington Harbor—defied Washington's color code by seating blacks and whites together, and it's been breaking ground ever since. One of the granddaddies of American regional theater, Arena has grown into a three-theater multiplex that specializes in productions long on political and theatrical courage (this is where *The Great White Hope* and *K2* originated years ago).

The brightest star of the edgy (in both the artistic and sociological sense) 14th Street Arts Corridor in Adams-Morgan, **Studio Theater** is actually Washington's third-largest producing company (after Shakespeare and the Arena). Founded in 1978 and renovated in 1997, Studio pays the rent with plays and musicals by contemporary heavyweights like David Mamet and Terrence McNally; longer runs get pushed upstairs to the smaller Secondstage, which also hosts "free of commercial consideration" envelope-pushers by upcoming theater artists.

The **Woolly Mammoth Theatre Company** on 14th Street has shelves full of Helen Hayes Awards (Washington's answer to Broadway's Tony) for groundbreaking premieres—local, regional, national—usually of the most shocking material they can get their hands on. Founded in 1987, the **Source Theatre Company** single-handedly brought culture to the 14th-and-U club ghetto. Recent hits have included Charles Busch's *Psycho Beach Party,* Harvey Fierstein's *Safe Sex,* the Washington premiere of *The Harvey Milk Show,* and brash revivals such as a *Merchant of Venice* played for laughs. Check out its off-hours programming for really out-there stuff. Mostly new work by playwrights of local and national repute, the Source's 70-play Washington Theatre Festival in July and August is the climax of otherwise virtually theaterless Washington summers.

The **District of Columbia Arts Center** (DCAC) in Adams-Morgan lends its stage to daring theatrical ventures by the likes of Fraudulent Productions and The Theater Conspiracy (patrons sometimes wish they hadn't), while its gallery houses exhibits like "Fetish: Elegant Objects of Seductive Obsession." Ongoing events include

Performance Improv Jams on the second Sunday of the month and DC Playback Theater, where the company reenacts personal life stories and historical events on third Sundays.

The Big Kahuna: Kennedy Center... Kennedy Center merits a category all its own, simply because Kennedy Center is in a class by itself. Between performances by resident companies, distinguished visitations, and productions that it mounts itself (Kennedy Center has co-produced more than 80 new shows, from feel-good musicals like *Annie* to the provocative drama *Angels In America*), Kennedy Center dominates Washington's performing-arts scene as does no institution in any other American city. Kennedy Center's territory consists of the middlebrow on up; the outer limits and rougher edges are left to lesser, un-federally subsidized institutions. Opened by order of Congress in 1971, Kennedy Center's six theaters host some 2,800 performances a year—music, theater, dance, and cinema. The recently rebuilt (and vastly improved) 2,750-seat Concert Hall is home to the **National Symphony Orchestra;** the **Washington Opera** invariably fills the 2,300 seats in the Opera House, which it shares with the **Washington Ballet.** Big-time musicals and brand-name plays are performed in the **Eisenhower Theater; Terrace Theater,** a gift from Japan, is the setting for chamber concerts and intimate theater works; and the **Theater Lab** presents children's programs and the audience-decides whodunit *Shear Madness,* which gets the award for sheer longevity—it opened in 1987 and still packs 'em in. The **American Film Institute Theater** screens Washington's artiest cinema—classic and contemporary films that seldom play elsewhere in town, with a different bill every day, up to four shows a day. The Center also offers free performances—from high-school glee clubs to jazz combos to string quartets—at 6pm nightly on the **Millennium Stage.** That's at the south end of the Grand Foyer, a room so vast that, sayeth Center publicity, "if the Washington Monument were laid on its side, it would fit inside the Grand Foyer with 75 feet to spare." Tip: Check out Kennedy Center's website (http://kennedy-center.org) for surfers-only discount deals.

Suburban stagecraft... Attending the theater in the D.C. suburbs these days means almost never having to say you're sorry—you skip the hassles of driving and parking in town, while you needn't fear wasting an evening on amateur night. Local audiences (always the last to know) are finally getting wind of some suburban troupes' national repute. The greater theatrical world (i.e., the *New York Times*) keeps its eye on the world premieres of groundbreaking musicals and plays at **Signature Theatre,** a 126-seat "black box" sequestered in a dramatically drab section of Arlington. Artistic director Eric Shaeffer, who can Sondheim with the best of them, is periodically summoned for assignments in New York. Also in Arlington, the **Gunston Arts Center** hosts a variety of pro companies: nervy old and new stuff by the American Century Theater (its recent rendition of Orson Welles's *Moby Dick Rehearsed* was a whale of a play); Horizon Theatre's cutting-edge work by and about women; and Hispanic plays and poetry readings in Spanish (simultaneous English translation sometimes available) by Teatro de la Luna.

Speaking freely at **George Mason University** Center for the Arts in Fairfax, the Theater of the First Amendment—motto "We Entertain Ideas"—stages plays about Contemporary American Life that often strike too close to home. A significant theatrical player long before this part of Maryland's Montgomery County was overtaken by suburban Washington sprawl, the nationally known **Olney Theatre Center** crams seven smartly staged productions onto its year-round Mainstage program, mostly modern American and English classics. **Round House Theatre,** which boasts the highest subscription renewal rate of any American theater, is a singlemindedly eclectic resident professional company expressing jaundiced—but funny—views of modern life. They started with *Godspell* in 1977, staged Pound's *Elektra, The Owl and the Pussycat,* and *The Belle of Amherst* along the way, and are reviving a new, improved *Godspell* in 1998.

Famous stages... Today **Ford's Theatre** looks exactly as it did the night of John Wilkes Booth's showstopping performance on April 14, 1865; you'd hardly believe that the house stood dark for over a century between then and Lincoln's birthday (February 12) in 1968. In the meantime, the federal government used the three-story structure for many nontheatrical functions: It was office space until it collapsed, killing 22 bureaucrats, in 1893, after which it was used for storage, and later as a museum until the grand restoration. Stage offerings here are still squeaky-clean and aggressively patriotic. The basement holds a small museum about the 19th-century theater and Lincoln; admission's free but it closes at 5pm.

Attached to the Daughters of the American Revolution (DAR) national headquarters, **DAR Constitution Hall** is most famous for a concert that never happened. After the Daughters canceled a scheduled gig by contralto Marian Anderson ("a Negress!"), First Lady Eleanor Roosevelt negotiated a freebie on the Mall—with the Lincoln Memorial as bandstand—that played to a crowd of 75,000. Now everyone plays Constitution Hall, from haughty harpists to raunchy rappers. On the other hand, African-Americans made the **Lincoln Theatre,** which opened in 1922, into the crown jewel of Washington's "Black Broadway," where Duke Ellington and Louis Armstrong came to play. It shut down in 1979, but reopened in 1993 as a municipally owned nonprofit facility dedicated to multicultural entertainment. It hosts the Smithsonian Jazz Masterworks Orchestra series, African and African-American dance ensembles, the Gay Men's Chorus of Washington, Hispanic folk groups, original plays, and an otherwise packed calendar of culturally diverse and artistically stellar performances.

It's academic: campus arts venues... Washington-area campus settings aren't noteworthy because of undergraduate talent, but because college auditoriums just happen to offer some of the largest spaces and best acoustics in the area. Most notably, George Washington University's **Lisner Auditorium** in D.C.'s Foggy Bottom neighborhood presents an eclectic array of pro talent—Joan Baez, Washington Concert Opera, chimp lady Jane Goodall, and tot idol Raffi, in recent seasons. Dimock Gallery, below the auditorium, displays changing exhibits on local themes. Fairfax County's answer to Kennedy Center is the multitheater Center for the Arts at **George Mason University.** A significant factor in the metro area's arts scene, GMU's ambitious and diverse schedule includes classical music (BBC Symphony, Academy of

St. Martin in the Fields), the Virginia Opera, contemporary dance troupes from around the world, jazz greats, bold plays by the Theater of the First Amendment, plus Movies at Mason—second-run American indies and only-run foreign flicks—Wednesday through Saturday. One of Washington's lesser-known gems, the In Series at tiny **Mount Vernon College** near Georgetown features dance, theater, opera, cabaret, and conversation in intimate Hand Chapel. In Rockville, Maryland, the **Montgomery College** Guest Artist Series features a mix of outside performers, from the Ballet Stars of Moscow to the Cambridge University Shakespeare players to the Ink Spots. Students and faculty are usually responsible (at least in this context) for hundreds of performances at **Georgetown University** each year—classical and jazz music, theater, poetry readings—at five campus venues for student-friendly prices ($5–$12). The arts season at **American University** in Northwest D.C. corresponds with the academic year, and the $5–$10 admissions correspond to academic budgets; expect an earnest melange of serious drama, musicals, experimental dance, and challenging choral works. **Catholic University of America** (CUA) in Northeast D.C.'s Catholic Bible Belt presents concerts by student-faculty groups plus guests, four plays a year, movies, and a series of lectures on not-necessarily religious subjects.

You hear a symphony... The major-league **National Symphony Orchestra** (NSO), revitalized when director Leonard Slatkin assumed the baton in 1996, plays over 100 concerts a year at Kennedy Center and fiddles away its summer at Wolf Trap and the Carter Barron Amphitheater. But the NSO isn't the only symphony in town, or even at Kennedy Center. The small, but in some respects more lovable, **Washington Chamber Symphony,** under Stephen Simon—Washington's version of Leonard Bernstein—offers "the intimate orchestral experience" at Kennedy Center's 500-seat Terrace Theater, Lisner Auditorium, and other venues about town. Outside city limits, the **Fairfax Symphony Orchestra** uses brand-name soloists to augment its own 98 musicians at the Center for the Arts at George Mason University and for the free Sounds of Summer concert series in Fairfax County parks. Since 1965, the **Washington Performing**

Arts Society has invited to town first-rate touring orchestras (Boston Symphony, Royal Philharmonic), superstar soloists and ensembles (Kathleen Battle, Itzhak Perlman, Wynton Marsalis, Alvin Ailey American Dance Theater), family concerts, performance-artist weirdness, and more, in venues from Kennedy Center and DAR Constitution Hall to the Washington National Cathedral and the GALA Hispanic Theatre. Check out their website (http://www.wpas.org) or call (see Index) for a schedule for the season.

Areas for arias... It's probably already too late to get tickets for any performances of the **Washington Opera**—over 95 percent of the seats for all its Kennedy Center performances are sold out before opening night, and they are particularly scarce when artistic director/tenor Placido Domingo takes the stage. It's easy to understand why: By blending superstar voices with local talent and alternating operatic chestnuts with lesser-known works and premieres, the seven ornate productions in the November–March season really bring out the "grand" in grand opera.

Don't hold high C waiting until the old Woodward & Lothrop department store downtown is transformed into the company's home stage—that won't happen until at least 2001. The next best choice is the **Opera Theater of Northern Virginia,** a resident company which performs three full-dress productions in English each season, plus a free outdoor summer show. One facet of the **Mount Vernon College** In Series consists of Opera in the Chapel—three fully staged professional experimental productions—including one Mozart birthday bash. The **Summer Opera Theatre Company** quite sensibly uses Catholic University's indoor Hartke Theater for two full-dress professional productions of opera standards.

Music, et cetera, in churches, et cetera... Divine acoustics make everybody sound great in **Washington National Cathedral**—the resident 210-voice Cathedral Choral Society as well as the many other groups that occasionally, but religiously, perform there. **St. John's Church** on Lafayette Square—the "Church of the Presidents" where every chief exec since Madison has attended services—hosts the **Washington Bach Consort**

for rush-hour concerts the last Tuesday of the month. This tightly knit and talented chamber ensemble's regular home is St. Paul's Lutheran Church in Northwest D.C. The **District of Columbia Jewish Community Center,** which has returned to its brilliantly restored original 1925 quarters in D.C. after nearly 30 years of diaspora in Rockville, Maryland, hosts thought-provoking and/or entertaining productions on Jewish issues by resident company Theater J. The **Jewish Community Center of Greater Washington** remains in Rockville, where a number of orchestral concerts are on the schedule; its resident Washington Jewish Theatre usually plays it for laughs, with schmaltzy performances but no ham acting. Other places of worship are also filled with the sound of music; find out where in the Thursday *Times* and the Friday *Post*.

Culture in other tongues... Considering how many foreign diplomats are quartered in Washington, you'd expect the town to have a flourishing foreign cultural scene—and it does. **GALA Hispanic Theatre** (GALA stands for Grupo de Actores Latino Americanos) in Adams-Morgan enjoys an Americas-wide reputation for classic and contemporary bilingual performances, plus Spanish-language dramas with simultaneous English translation. **Le Néon French-American Theatre,** a professional troupe headquartered in Arlington, maintains language barriers and eschews simultaneous translation: French plays and dramatizations of French literary works are performed either in English or in French. **La Maison Française** offers a golden opportunity to infiltrate the striking French embassy in Georgetown for French plays and lectures (in French), French films with English subtitles, concerts, and art exhibits; some are free, all are well worth your time. The **Goethe Institute** serves copious portions of *der deutschen Kulturszene*—quasi-official German cinema, theater, music, dance, literature—in its expansive new headquarters on the fringe of D.C.'s Chinatown. The nonprofessional **British Embassy Players** mount five jolly good shows a year in the embassy rotunda, including, each spring, an utterly smashing Old Time Music Hall. The **Embassy Series** offers a movable feast of concerts appropriate to the host venue—for example, an "Homage to Clara and Robert Schumann" at the German Embassy. The best place to find out about the many one-shot—and usually free—lectures, concerts, films, and plays presented at various embassies is the *Post's* Weekend section.

Gotta dance... Dance is not one of Washington's cultural strengths; what could dance possibly say that couldn't be better expressed by a 1,200-page position paper? There just isn't much dance, and what there is tends to stick safely to the middle of the stage. The itinerant and versatile **Washington Ballet** company performs a fall, winter, and spring series at Kennedy Center, takes over Warner Theater for the *Nutcracker* season, and occasionally pirouettes onto other local stages. **Kennedy Center,** which hosted the American debuts of the Bolshoi Ballet and the Ballet Nacional de Cuba, welcomes the world's top visiting troupes from October through mid-May. The **Washington Performing Arts Society** devotes two of its many series specifically to dance—Dance All Over and Dance at Dance Place—and also features visiting world-class talent in some other series. **Dance Place** itself is a school and showplace for modern dance with "culturally specific" (African, African-American, gay, gay African-American) performances throughout the year; top locals and respected visiting troupes perform here. **Prince George's Publick Playhouse** in Hyattsville, Maryland, hosts resident companies of various skill levels for multicultural dance programming.

Picture palaces and cinemas... Cinema-wise, Washington lags behind New York, Chicago, San Francisco, and L.A., but exceeds almost every place else. Although multiplexes and multiplex-minded programming dominate, almost every worthy independent domestic film and import gets its Washington run. However, if you're out of town that day you might miss it. The main event in Washington's cinematic calendar is **Filmfest DC**: Ten days of carefully selected international delights—including a bunch of freebies—at a half-dozen venues all over town. These are the sorts of films that aren't likely to nail a theatrical run in Washington the rest of the year. Filmfest DC doesn't rank with the New York Film Festival or Cannes in terms of volume, prestige, or civic prominence, but it gets bigger and better every year. Washington's top (and really only) art house is the four-screen **Key Theatre** in Georgetown; the **American Film Institute Theater** in Kennedy Center shows offbeat new films or revivals, but its constantly changing schedule (a different film every night) means you've got to hustle right over if they're showing something you particularly want to see. Much the same goes for the Movies at Mason series at the Center for the Arts at **George Mason University** out in Fairfax, Virginia, where a Wednesday–Saturday schedule offers intriguing American independent movies and some foreign films.

The **Cineplex Odeon Dupont Circle** presents challenging domestic and imported films, but its screens are oh-so-tiny. You want big screens? We got big screens. The restored **Cineplex Odeon Uptown** in Cleveland Park brings back the days when movie theaters were movie theaters, with a wraparound, battleship-sized screen that, even from the balcony, can add a star and a half to the boisterous Hollywood blockbusters that usually run. The screen at Theater 1 (of two) at the **Cineplex Odeon Avalon** is nearly as vast, and the films shown here tend to be more thoughtful, sometimes even foreign. The **AMC Union Station 9,** in the catacombs beneath Union Station, is the closest thing in D.C. to a suburban multiplex: Each of its nine screens is named for a different Washington theater of yore.

Washington's best movie bargain is the five-screen **Cineplex Odeon Foundry** in Georgetown, which shows foreign films and American indies for $2.50 a seat, any time of day. As you may gather, the odious Cineplexing of Washington is in full swing, which does have one advantage: online, one-stop shopping for info on what's showing at all of D.C.'s many Cineplex Odeons at http://www.cineplexodeon.com.

Free verse... Washington boasts—or at least tolerates—a vibrant and eclectic poetry scene, where you'll find plenty of the three pillars of modern American poetry: academic poets, workshop poets, and urban poets. D.C. even has something of a Poets' Corner—14th and U streets, in the edgy nightlife district where some clubs, shops, and galleries host free or cheap readings, usually on weeknights with weeknight-level, modest crowds. A prime site here is the **Ruthless Grip,** a row-house co-op art gallery that features local, national, and international poets one Saturday night every month, with an arty emphasis on the experimental and the avant-garde. **Atticus Books,** a politically progressive bookstore on the ground floor of the same building, also hosts readings on a more irregular basis, with angry young poets reading their work with suitable passion. Nearby **Mango's** restaurant hosts regular Tuesday night open readings, with tea and sympathy for neophytes. Sensitive young grungesters alternate with tribal rapsters to produce sound and fury in the name of poetic justice. Elsewhere, the New Words Coffeehouse Series at the **Writer's Center** out in Bethesda offers something literary—poetry, prose, play readings, storytelling, improv—and opportunities for audience members to form couplets every Friday night. Washington's most, well, *poetic* poetry event is the free **Joaquin Miller Cabin Poetry Series** in June and July, an outdoor reading by nationally known poets and promising newcomers beside the "Poet of the Sierras" transplanted shack in Rock Creek Park. The audience arrives by foot, car, or bike, often accompanied by children and pets. Afterward, you're invited to a reception in the home of noted local poetess Jacklyn Potter. Poetry breaks out all the time at area bookstores, coffeehouses, galleries, museums, and libraries; check listings in the Friday *Post* (On stage: Literary Readings) or *Paper* (Events: Readings/Literature) to ascertain whither and whence.

Theater on the menu... Dinner theaters around here are pretty much in a theatrical time warp—if they've gained some retro cachet, it's only in the sense that people who used to do retro got old enough to actually like them. In other words, they're so out they're still out. **West End Dinner Theatre** in Alexandria serves up repertory American musicals (*Bye Bye Birdie, Little Shop of Horrors*) along with special-events concerts resuscitating the likes of Glenn Miller and Elvis. Its chief distinction is that it serves sit-down meals—standard American fare with several entrée choices—rather than a buffet. At the **Burn Brae Dinner Theater** in Burtonsville, Maryland, musical comedies and hum-alongable reviews work up appetites for the tasty bottomless buffet—salmon in dill sauce, veal parmigiana, turkey breast, and all the usual salads. Head south to the **Lazy Susan Dinner Theater** in Woodbridge, Virginia, for the Pennsylvania Dutch buffet—copious quantities of roast beef, chicken, fish, salads, and desserts, all made from scratch. The accompanying theatrical fare includes musicals, mysteries, and musical mysteries. **Toby's Dinner Theatre,** halfway between Washington and Baltimore, augments Broadway chestnuts with new musicals (recently, a spoof called *Phantom of the Country Palace,* set at the Grand Ole Opry) and a vast buffet with a make-your-own sundae bar. The butler (and chef and waiter) have been doing it since 1988 at the **Blair Mansion Inn Murder Mystery Dinner Theater,** where an interactive murder mystery is staged with all-you-can-eat buffet (roast beef, chicken, fish, etc.) and cash bar. If nothing else, the setting is impressive—a 110-year-old Stanford White–designed mansion that's allegedly haunted. Founded in 1986, **Mystery on the Menu** was Washington's first interactive mystery dinner theater—audience members get to play good cop/bad cop—and it's still the only one within District limits. **Dave and Buster's Dinner Mystery Theatre** serves sit-down meals and mystery in stages: Act 1, Crime/Caesar Salad; Act II, Suspects Assemble/Entrée; Act III, Mystery Solved/Dessert. The dinner/mystery package is just one item featured here, along with bars, restaurant, billiards, video games, fun casino, simulators, all in a North Bethesda adult playground.

Stars beneath the stars... The only American national park devoted to the performing arts, **Wolf Trap** is the best and probably only reason to endure Washington summers. Situated in suburban Virginia between the Beltway and Dulles Airport, Wolf Trap seats some 4,000 bodies within the park's Filene Center and offers a grassy knoll with stage views (lawn chairs to the rear, please) to 3,000 more. Wolf Trap books the best in every musical genre, and great acoustics make the absence of a roof no sound barrier. The **National Symphony Orchestra** plays about a dozen times during the late-May to early-September season, but music-wise anything goes at Wolf Trap, from Ray Charles to Willie Nelson to (reputed extraterrestrial) John Tesh. Seasonal standbys include the Irish Folk Festival in May, Louisiana Swamp Romp and the Jazz & Blues Festival in June, Live Film Festival (movies accompanied by NSO) in July, opera and musicals in August. Picnics strongly encouraged.

Within the District, **Carter Barron Amphitheater** in Rock Creek Park is the invigorating setting for the Shakespeare Theater's Shakespeare Free-for-All for two weeks in June. The rest of the summer it offers free and National Symphony Orchestra performances and not-free jazz (Herbie Hancock, Wayne Shorter, D.C. Jazzmania in 1997), gospel, pop, and R&B concerts. Halfway to Baltimore, the **Merriweather Post Pavilion** attracts mainly the young for headline rock, rap, and country acts, plus some oldies. Halfway to Kentucky (it's actually just past Manassas, but traffic moves slowly), the **Nissan Pavilion at Stone Ridge** is the newest and hugest venue (10,000 sheltered seats under a stark, exposed-steel pavilion, 15,000 on the sloping turf) for classical/pop/rock/soul/jazz/country performances; the Who, Tina Turner, Aerosmith, James Taylor, and Lollapalooza turned up in 1997. The **Armed Forces Concert Series** is something you sure can't get in any other town: uniformed bands from all four branches of the service performing marches, patriotic anthems, light classics, and big-band hits. Sites and nights vary, but you can count on seeing some group of proficient uniformed musicians at either the Sylvan Theater on the Washington Monument grounds or the East Terrace of the U.S. Capitol every night except Saturday, from June through August. These guys and gals are *good,* and there's something wonderful in a dopey way about hearing a crack brass band play outdoors of a summer's eve.

Rock 'n' pop concert zones... **Kennedy Center** occasionally books top jazz and pop acts. When Sinatra-class show-biz equivalents of national monuments tour, they grace the grand stage of the totally renovated 1924 **Warner Theater.** The biddies who in 1939 vetoed Marian Anderson's concert at **DAR Constitution Hall** would surely blush to see their hallowed premises occasionally invaded these days by acts like the Freak Like Me Tour ("For Mature Audiences Only") and multiracial pop acts, among more sedate performances. Reopened in 1994 after a $9 million renovation, the **Lincoln Theatre,** a 1921 movie theater and vaudeville house in the heart of the U Street entertainment district, highlights African-American plays, dance, and music; non-black acts (the Average White Band, for instance) also appear.

Campus concert halls—**Lisner Auditorium** at George Washington University and Bender Arena at **American University**—specialize in progressive rock groups with toes in the mainstream. Out in the suburbs, sports arenas periodically lend their cavernous spaces to pop/rock/rap acts that think they can fill them—all 20,000 seats at **USAirways Arena,** an unlovable building on an unappealing off-Beltway site without a whisper of public transportation in Landover, Maryland; and 9,500 seats at **George Mason University**'s Patriot Center out in Fairfax, Virginia. Some of that action has now shifted to **MCI Arena,** which opened downtown in the fall of 1997.

The Arts: Index

Note: Where no Metro stop is supplied, a venue is best reached by taxi or car.

AMC Union Station 9. Subterranean multiplex screens the usual first-run suspects.... *Tel 703/998–4AMC. First St. at Massachusetts Ave., NE. Union Station Metro.* **(see p. 95)**

American Film Institute (AFI) Theater. Kennedy Center's palais du cinema features the best offbeat foreign and domestic films, plus revivals. Up to four films a day; programs change daily.... *Tel 202/785–4600. Kennedy Center, New Hampshire Ave. at Rock Creek Pkwy., NW. Foggy Bottom-GWU Metro (free shuttle from 9:45am–midnight Mon–Sat, noon–midnight Sun and holidays).* **(see pp. 88, 95)**

American University. The performing-arts department casts student and faculty talent in drama, dance, and choral music.... *Tel 202/885–ARTS (info), 202/885–2587. 4400 Massachusetts Ave., NW. Tenleytown Metro.* **(see pp. 91, 99)**

Arena Stage. Groundbreaking regional theater entertains a quarter-million patrons per September–June season in a three-stage complex south of the Capitol.... *Tel 202/488–4377, TTY 202/484–0247, http://www.shirenet.com/arena-stage. 6th St. at Maine Ave., SW. Waterfront Metro.* **(see p. 87)**

Armed Forces Concert Series. Free outdoor performances at on- and off-Mall sites June–Aug, indoor concerts year-round.... *Tel 202/767–5658 (Air Force), 703/696–3399 (Army), 202/433–4011 (Marines), 202/433–2525 (Navy).* **(see p. 98)**

Atticus Books. Hosts occasional poetry readings.... *Tel 202/667–8148. 1508 U St., NW. U Street-Cardozo Metro.* **(see p. 96)**

Blair Mansion Inn Murder Mystery Dinner Theatre. Hundred-percent interactive performances and buffet meals in an August 19th-century edifice on the D.C.-Maryland borderline.... *Tel 301/588–6646. 7711 Eastern Ave., Silver Spring, MD. Fri–Sun.* **(see p. 97)**

British Embassy Players. Ripping good plays enacted by embassy staffers.... *Tel 703/271–0172. British Embassy Rotunda, 3100 Massachusetts Ave., NW.* **(see p. 93)**

Burn Brae Dinner Theater. Feel-good musicals, fill-good buffet.... *Tel 301/384–5800. 3811 Blackburn Rd., Burtonsville, MD.* **(see p. 96)**

Carter Barron Amphitheater. A sylvan glade in Rock Creek Park provides the setting for classical and pop concerts and plays, some of them free, throughout the summer.... *Tel 202/260–6837. 16th St. at Colorado Ave., NW.* **(see p. 98)**

Catholic University of America. Students, faculty, and guest artists perform concerts and plays year-round; (indoor) summer opera series.... *Tel 202/319–5000. 620 Michigan Ave., NE. Brookland-CUA Metro.* **(see p. 91)**

Cineplex Odeon Avalon. Big screen downstairs, mini-screen above, lots of indies and foreign films in Chevy Chase, D.C.... *Tel 202/333–FILM, #787. 5612 Connecticut Ave., NW.* **(see p. 95)**

Cineplex Odeon Dupont Circle. Films of substance on five dinky screens.... *Tel 202/333–FILM, #792. 1350 19th St., NW. Dupont Circle Metro.* **(see p. 95)**

Cineplex Odeon Foundry. Georgetown art house with bargain rates for second-run indies and imports.... *Tel 202/333–FILM, #827. 1055 Thomas Jefferson St., NW. Foggy Bottom–GWU Metro.* **(see p. 95)**

Cineplex Odeon Uptown. A huge screen, monster sound, and a cozy balcony add up to D.C.'s favorite movie house.... *Tel*

202/333–FILM, #799. 3426 Connecticut Ave., NW. Cleveland Park Metro. **(see p. 95)**

Dance Place. Northeast Brookland neighborhood school and 199-seat performance space for eclectic contemporary dance programs.... *Tel 202/269–1600. 3225 8th St., NE. Brookland-CUA Metro.* **(see p. 94)**

DAR Constitution Hall. A grand setting and terrific acoustics for the gamut of classical, pop, rock, and rap performances.... *Tel 202/638–2661. 18th St. between C and D sts., NW. Farragut West Metro.* **(see pp. 90, 98)**

Dave & Buster's Dinner Mystery Theatre. Play's the thing—in every conceivable configuration—at this adult amusement center with three-act mystery dinner.... *Tel 301/230–5151. White Flint Mall, 11301 Rockville Pike, N. Bethesda, MD. White Flint Metro. Fri–Sat.* **(see p. 97)**

District of Columbia Arts Center (DCAC). Adams-Morgan performance space/gallery presents its own cutting-edge shows and lends its stage to outsiders (in every sense of the word).... *Tel 202/462–7833. 2438 18th St., NW. Woodley Park–Zoo Metro.* **(see p. 87)**

District of Columbia Jewish Community Center. Restored Coolidge-era facility presents plays and musicals on Jewish themes, plus movies and concerts. Valet parking at Q Street entrance; free shuttles from Dupont Metro.... *Tel 202/518–9400. 16th St. at Q St., NW. Dupont Circle Metro.* **(see p. 93)**

Embassy Series. Five classical music concerts at five European embassies—with artist receptions afterwards.... *Tel 202/625–2361. P.O. Box 9871, Washington D.C. 20016. Nov–May.* **(see p. 93)**

Eisenhower Theater. See Kennedy Center.

Fairfax Symphony Orchestra. Forty years old in 1997, they play the classics and pops at George Mason University, but frequently go on the road.... *Tel 703/642–7200, fax 703/642–7205. P. O. Box 1300, Annandale, VA, 22003.* **(see p. 91)**

Filmfest DC. Ten-day late-April/early-May movie marathon. Locations vary from year to year; advance tickets available from Protix.... *Tel 202/628–FILM, fax 202/724–6578. P. O. Box 21396, Washington D.C. 20009.* **(see p. 94)**

Ford's Theatre. Historic, painstakingly restored setting for family-oriented musicals, bios of "American originals," and Dickens's A Christmas Carol every holiday season... *Tel 202/347–4833, TTY 202/347–5599. 511 10th St., NW. Metro Center or Gallery Place–Chinatown Metros.*

(see pp. 86, 89)

GALA Hispanic Theatre . Spanish—with simultaneous translation—and English-language productions of contemporary and classic Latin American and Spanish plays. Free parking—a boon in Adams-Morgan.... *Tel 202/234-7174. 1625 Park Rd., NW.* **(see p. 93)**

George Mason University. Four-theater Center for the Arts complex on GMU's main campus brings the cream of the performing crop to the wilds of northern Virginia. Patriot Center athletics stadium also hosts concerts.... *Tel 703/993–8888, http://www.gmu.edu/cfa. Rte. 123 at Braddock Rd., Fairfax, VA.* **(see pp. 89, 90, 95, 99)**

Georgetown University. Busy season of low-cost plays, classical music, and jazz at various campus venues close to Georgetown restaurants and nightlife.... Center for the Arts: *Tel 202/687–6783. 37th St. at O St., NW (campus entrance). Patriot Center: Tel 703/993–3000. 4400 University Dr., Fairfax, VA.* **(see p. 91)**

Goethe Institute. The D.C. bastion of worldwide Teutonic culture presents German films, plays, music, literature.... *Tel 202/289–1200. 814 7th St., NW. Gallery Place–Chinatown Metro.* **(see p. 93)**

Gunston Arts Center. Arlington County Cultural Affairs Division facility, used by several theater and dance groups.... *Tel 703/358–6960. 2700 South Lang St., Arlington, VA.*

(see p. 89)

Jewish Community Center of Greater Washington. Washington Jewish Theatre does mostly Jewish-themed

musicals. Also J.C.C. Symphony Orchestra concerts, chamber-music series.... *Tel 301/230–3775. 6125 Montrose Rd., Rockville, MD.* **(see p. 93)**

Joaquin Miller Cabin Poetry Series. Eight outdoor readings by established bards and neophytes in June–July season. Tuesdays at 7:30pm; call for rain location.... *Tel 202/726–0971. Rock Creek Park, Beach Dr. north of Military Rd. overpass.* **(see p. 96)**

Kennedy Center. Washington's one-stop cultural category-killer has six theaters of various sizes, configurations, and grandiosity. Home to the **National Symphony Orchestra,** the **Washington Opera,** the **Washington Ballet,** the **American Film Institute,** and much, much more. Paid underground parking.... *Tel 202/467–4600, 800/444– 1324, TDD 202/416–8524, http://kennedy-center.org. New Hampshire Ave. at Rock Creek Pkwy., NW. Foggy Bottom–GWU Metro (free shuttle 9:45am–midnight Mon–Sat, noon–midnight Sun and holidays).* **(see pp. 88, 91, 94, 97, 98)**

Key Theatre. The last of the independent art houses in Georgetown, with midnight showings on weekends.... *Tel 202/333–5100. 1222 Wisconsin Ave., NW. Foggy Bottom–GWU Metro.* **(see p. 95)**

La Maison Française. French drama (in French), film, music, and art offer diplomatic impunity to visit the French embassy.... *Tel 202/944–6091. Embassy of France, 4101 Reservoir Rd., NW.* **(see p. 93)**

Lazy Susan Dinner Theater. Mostly musicals and groaning buffet at 20-year-old showplace theoretically 20 minutes south of downtown Washington.... *Tel 703/550–7384, http://www.lazysusan.com. I-95 at U.S. 1, Woodbridge, VA.* **(see p. 96)**

Le Néon French-American Theatre. French-only and alternating French and English productions of classic and modern French texts.... *Tel 703/243–6366. 3616 Lee Highway, Arlington, VA. Virginia Square Metro.* **(see p. 93)**

Lincoln Theatre. Restored remnant of D.C.'s Black Broadway, once again the hot ticket for multicultural entertainment in

the U Street Corridor.... *Tel 202/328–6000. 1215 U St., NW. U Street-Cardozo Metro.* **(see pp. 90, 98)**

Lisner Auditorium. George Washington University campus facility in Foggy Bottom serves as major non–Kennedy Center venue for world-class performing arts professionals and student shows.... *Tel 202/994–1500, http://gwu. edu/~lisner. 21st St. at I St., NW. Foggy Bottom–GWU Metro.* **(see pp. 90, 99)**

Mango's. U Street Corridor eatery with open-mike poetry Tuesdays 8–10pm. Dollar cover waived for readers.... *Tel 202/332–2104. 2017 14th St., NW. U Street–Cardozo Metro.* **(see p. 96)**

MCI Arena. Downtown home of b-ball Wizards and hockey's Capitals hosts rock concerts on off nights.... *601 F St., NW. Gallery Place-Chinatown Metro.* **(see p. 99)**

Merriweather Post Pavilion. Amphitheater in 50-acre park hosts new pop/rock/rap/country stars and golden oldies.... *Tel 301/982–1800, 800/955–5566, TDD 410/730–2345, http://www.mppconcerts.com. 10475 South Entrance Rd. (off U.S. 29), Columbia, MD.* **(see p. 98)**

Millennium Stage. See Kennedy Center.

Montgomery College. The Guest Artist Series brings a world of talent to Maryland's second most populous city.... *Tel 301/279–5301. 51 Manakee St., Rockville, MD.* **(see p. 91)**

Mount Vernon College. In Series ranges from opera to poetry jams; the Women's Work, Woman's Words Festival crops up in March.... *Tel 202/625–4655. 2100 Foxhall Rd., NW (enter on W St.).* **(see pp. 91, 92)**

Mystery on the Menu. Regular Saturday night whodunit dinners at D.C.'s Old Europe Restaurant; inquire for particulars of special performances throughout the Washington/Baltimore crime scene..... *Tel 202/333–6875. Old Europe, 2434 Wisconsin Ave., NW. Sat.* **(see p. 97)**

National Symphony Orchestra. See Kennedy Center.

The National Theatre. The fifth rewrite of America's oldest touring house features big-ticket musicals on their way to or just coming from Broadway.... *Tel 202/628–6161, 800/447–7400, http://www.nationaltheatre.org. 1321 Pennsylvania Ave., NW. Metro Center Metro.* **(see p. 86)**

Nissan Pavilion at Stone Ridge. Variety of summer entertainment with seating under the stars or the roof of the monster pavilion.... *Tel 703/754–6400. 7800 Cellar Door Rd. (off I-66 at U.S. 29), Bristow, VA.* **(see p. 98)**

Olney Theatre Center. Montgomery County's 50-year-old mainstay produces seven plays a year for adults, plus kids' shows.... *Tel 301/924–3400. 2001 Olney–Sandy Spring Rd., Olney, MD.* **(see p. 89)**

Opera Theatre of Northern Virginia. Professional troupe mounts three costumed indoor productions a season, usually in various locations in Arlington, plus one free outdoor summer production.... *Tel 703/528–1433. Mailing address: 4736 Lee Hwy., Arlington, VA 22207.* **(see p. 92)**

Prince George's Publick Playhouse. Home base for multicultural dance companies and others, with a 462-seat proscenium stage.... *Tel 301/277–1710, TTY 301/277-0312. 5445 Landover Rd., Cheverly, MD.* **(see p. 94)**

Round House Theatre. Resident pros at 20-year-old Montgomery County stage act out witty, mature-minded takes on contemporary existence.... *Tel 301/933–1644. Veirs Mill Rd. at Randolph Rd., Silver Spring, MD.* **(see p. 89)**

Ruthless Grip. Artist-owned gallery runs monthly poetry readings on the second Saturday of the month (except July and August) at 7:30pm.... *Tel 202/637–0441. 1508 U St., NW. U Street–Cardozo Metro.* **(see p. 95)**

St. John's Church. Free Rush Hour Concert Series on the last Tuesday of the month in a historic church across from the White House.... *Tel 202/337–1202. 16th St. at H St., NW. McPherson Square or Farragut North Metro.* **(see p. 92)**

Shakespeare Theatre. Count on three worthy renderings of the Bard in a five-play indoor season, plus the Shakespeare Free-for-All in Rock Creek Park each June.... *Tel 202/393–2700, http://shakespearedc.org. 450 7th St., NW. Gallery Place or Archives Metro. Sept–June.* **(see p. 86)**

Signature Theatre. Mostly musicals, but new, edgy ones including Sondheim-acclaimed renditions of Sondheim.... *Tel 703/820–9771. 3806 S. Four Mile Run Dr., Arlington, VA.* **(see p. 89)**

Source Theatre Company. Hundred-seat setting for multicultural interpretations of new work and classics, a 10-minute-play summer festival, and the extra-weird Off Hours series. Pay-what-you-can previews and free play readings. Free valet parking Friday and Saturday nights.... *Tel 202/462–1073. 1835 14th St., NW. U Street–Cardozo Metro.* **(see p. 87)**

Studio Theatre. Renovated two-stage complex mingles old and new plays downstairs, bold new experiments in drama and performance art above.... *Tel 202/332–3300, http://www.studiotheatre.org. 1333 P St., NW. Dupont Circle Metro.* **(see p. 87)**

Summer Opera Theater Company. Two classic operas, fully staged and professionally performed in an air-conditioned indoor theater.... *Tel 202/319–4000. Hartke Theatre, Catholic University of America, 3801 Harewood Rd., NE. Brookland-CUA Metro.* **(see p. 92)**

Terrace Theater. See Kennedy Center.

Theater Lab. See Kennedy Center.

Toby's Dinner Theatre. The area's only dinner-theater-in-the-round offers family-friendly musicals and buffet dinners.... *Tel 301/596–6161, 800/88–TOBYS. South Entrance Rd., Columbia, MD.* **(see p. 97)**

USAirways Arena. Sports stadium doubles as rock arena.... *Tel 301/622–3865. 1 N. Harry S Truman Dr., Landover, MD.* **(see p. 99)**

Warner Theater. Downtown Art Deco showplace for Broadway road shows and top headliner concerts.... *Tel 202/783–4000, 800/669–STAGE, http://www.warnertheatre.com. 13th St. at Pennsylvania Ave., NW. Metro Center Metro.* **(see pp. 86, 98)**

Washington Bach Consort. Go for baroque at the regular season in St. Paul's Lutheran Church and other sacred settings.... *Tel 202/337–1202. St. Paul's Lutheran Church, 4900 36th St., NW. Oct–May.* **(see p. 92)**

Washington Ballet. No home stage, but the versatile company occupies Kennedy Center for three yearly "seasons," as well as Warner Theatre and George Mason Arts Center.... *Tel 202/362–3606. Mailing address: 3515 Wisconsin Ave., NW 20016.* **(see pp. 88, 94)**

Washington Chamber Symphony. Second string at Kennedy Center—after the NSO—but first-rate at the Corcoran Gallery, Lisner Auditorium, and everywhere else they perform.... *Tel 202/452–1321. 1099 22nd St., NW, Washington D.C. 20037. Oct–May.* **(see p. 91)**

Washington National Cathedral. Home base for the venerable Cathedral Choral Society and transient classical performers.... *Tel 202/537–8980 (Choral Society), 202/537–6200 (information), http://www.cathedral. org./cathedral. Wisconsin Ave. at Massachusetts Ave., NW.* **(see p. 92)**

Washington Opera. Seven major-league productions a year at Kennedy Center, almost always sold out. Returned tickets may be available at the box office an hour before curtain.... *Tel 202/416–7800, 800/87–OPERA, http://www.dc-opera.org. Kennedy Center, New Hampshire Ave. at Rock Creek Pkwy., NW. Foggy Bottom–GWU Metro (free shuttle from 9:45am–midnight Mon–Sat, noon–midnight Sun and holidays). Nov–Mar.* **(see pp. 88, 92)**

Washington Performing Arts Society. The WPAS produces a dozen or so annual series—mostly classical but also jazz, dance, and world music—in performance sites grand and intimate around D.C.... *Tel 202/833–9800, TDD 202/467–6922, http://www.wpas.org. Mailing address: 2000 L St., NW, Suite 810 20036-4907.* **(see pp. 91, 94)**

Washington Stage Guild. Historic Carroll Hall is the downtown setting for classic plays, most of which you've never heard of.... *Tel 202/529–2084. Carroll Hall, 924 G St., NW. Gallery Place or Metro Center Metro. Oct–May.* **(see p. 86)**

West End Dinner Theatre. Tuneful dinner-theater standbys and oldies concerts served with a menu of sit-down options.... *Tel 703/370–2500, http://www.wedt.com. 4615 Duke St., Alexandria, VA.* **(see p. 96)**

Wolf Trap. Summer outdoor season includes the best of every kind of music plus dance, theater, even movies. Seating under and behind Filene Center pavilion. Order gourmet picnics for pickup at Wolf Trap (tel 703/319–2000, ask for "Wolf Trap catering"). The rest of the year, folk, jazz, and chamber-music concerts are performed indoors at the nearby Barns of Wolf Trap.... *Tel 703/255–1827, 703/218–6500 (Protix), TDD 703/218–9432, http://www.wolf-trap.org. 1624 Trap Rd., Vienna, VA. Shuttle from West Fall Church Metro (Orange Line) from 2 hours before performance time. Late May–mid-Sept.* **(see p. 97)**

Woolly Mammoth Theatre Company. Ensemble company spotlights innovative work exploring critical political, interpersonal, and social issues. Free attended parking opposite entrance. Pay-what-you-can previews.... *Tel 202/393–3939. 1401 Church St., NW. Dupont Circle Metro.* **(see p. 87)**

Writer's Center. Friday night Coffeehouse opens mike to poets, prosers, songwriters, tale-tellers—with receptions after words. Check out their website for literary events elsewhere.... *Tel 301/654–8664, http://writer.org. 4508 Walsh St., Bethesda, MD. Bethesda Metro.* **(see p. 96)**

spo

rts 4

Politics is the real spectator sport around Washington, and in many ways the chief recreational sport as well. The city is full of Type-A lawyers who pack their legal briefs with buns of steel—you can see them out running and biking and power-walking at 6am when you're stumbling home (ask the cab driver to veer over near the curb and maybe you can wing one with the door)—but it's definitely a thing people do to succeed, not to have fun. And they do it by day, not at night. There's not a single 24-hour gym, bowling alley, or miniature golf course in the District of Columbia. Few hotels have pools, and even fewer are big enough for lap swimming. After dark, recreating Washingtonians are more likely to find themselves under bar stools than barbells.

There *is* one thing that unites Washington's starkly divergent populations: the Redskins. The capital's NFL team—which has won three (and lost two) Super Bowls—is so popular that all its games have been sold out since the late sixties; there are 49,000 names on the waiting list for season tickets (divorce battles over season tickets are the stuff of local legend). But the truth is that during subpar Redskins season, there are a striking number of no-shows in those season seats. This is a town that loves only winners.

Washington is just not that much of a sports town. There's no rabid tabloid newspaper that rips every coaching decision or boneheaded play. Sports talk–radio barely exists; the one all-sports radio station (WTEM, AM 570) seems like it has the broadcast range of a guy with a megaphone. The two daily newspapers—the *Washington Post* and the *Washington Times*—give the fans what they want: exhaustive, often boosterish Redskins coverage. The *Post* arguably has one of the top sports sections in America, long on nuts-and-bolts sports stuff, event coverage, and strong writing. The much smaller *Times* doesn't cover other sports as thoroughly as it covers the Skins, which it does quite well. (It didn't hurt that the Redskins' owner, the late Jack Kent Cooke, refused to grant interviews to the *Post*, having reportedly taken offense at the paper's decision to cover the Baltimore Ravens, not to mention a 1996 editorial that called him "egomaniacal.")

Venues and Tickets

Sports tickets can be had directly from the teams themselves or through **TicketMaster** (tel 202/432–SEAT). Ticket brokers (**Ticket Finders**, tel 301/927–8000; **Top Centre Ticket Service**, tel 202/452–9040) procure tickets to most sporting events, but the markups can be enormous. Starting with the 1997–98 season, the NHL's Caps and the NBA's Wizards (née Bullets) left the **USAirways Arena** in suburban

Maryland (1 N. Harry S Truman Dr., Landover, MD) for brand-new high-tech **MCI Center** in downtown Washington (601 F St., NW). They were passed in transit by the Redskins, who left **RFK Stadium** in the District (2400 E. Capitol St., SE) for the new 78,600-seat **Jack Kent Cooke Stadium** out in Raljon, Maryland (a Cooke-created fiefdom whose name combines those of Cooke's two sons). It's a couple of Beltway exits south of the USAirways Arena. The D.C. United soccer team continues to use RFK Stadium; the Washington Warthogs (indoor soccer) and the Georgetown Hoyas (college basketball) still play at the USAirways Arena.

Up in Baltimore, the Ravens football team plays on in the friendly confines of **Memorial Stadium** (1000 E. 33rd. St., Baltimore, MD), the storied home of the Johnny Unitas–era Colts, set in a Baltimore row-house neighborhood. But not for long: In 1998 the Ravens are due to move into a new stadium being built on the D.C. side of Baltimore, adjacent to the Orioles' **Camden Yards** ballpark (333 W. Camden St., Baltimore, MD). Opened in 1992, Camden Yards was built to look like an old ballpark, with real grass, an open center-field view of downtown, and even a renovated red-brick B&O Railroad warehouse beyond the right-field fence.

The Lowdown

Where to watch

Second down and goal to go... Pro football is not really a nighttime sport, save for the exhibition season and a couple nights a year when the team is slated to appear on "Monday Night Football." Getting tickets to watch the **Washington Redskins** (tel 202/546–2222) is nearly impossible anyway, even in the new stadium out in Raljon, Maryland, south of the USAirways Arena. If you're desperately in need of a Redskins fix, you can access Redskins info online at http://nflhome.com/teams/redskins/redskins.html. A 45-minute drive up Interstate 95 to Baltimore, however, will take you to Memorial Stadium, home of the **Baltimore Ravens** (tel 410/654–6247). Yes, the name is an homage to Edgar Allen Poe, who died destitute in Baltimore in 1849. The Ravens, formerly the Cleveland Browns, moved to Baltimore before the 1996 season, finally replacing the long-lamented Baltimore Colts, who stole out of town in 1984 to new stables in Indianapolis. Single-game tickets are generally available for Ravens games.

Stealing home... Thanks to a longer season and more frequent games, pro baseball offers fans many more spectating chances, most of them at night games. But ever since the Washington Senators abandoned the city (*twice*, in fact—in 1960 the original Senators became the Minnesota Twins; in 1971 the expansion-team Senators became the Texas Rangers), Washington has pined for a team of its own. But the curse of *Damn Yankees* (in which a fan of the hapless Senators makes a deal with the devil so that his team can beat the fearsome Yanks... and then renegs) continues to hover over the city as the devil gets his due and team after team passes the city by. The San Diego Padres almost moved here. Then the Houston Astros. Cities like Phoenix and Tampa/St. Petersburg got expansion teams, as the Center of the Free World was passed over again and again. So baseball-starved fans did the next best thing: They grudgingly adopted the **Baltimore Orioles** (tel 410/547–6234), not to mention the team's durable superstar Cal Ripken, who hasn't missed a game since 1983. The up side is that Camden Yards, the O's stadium, is only a 30-minute drive up I-95 from Washington. The Orioles are often sold out, but single-game tickets (there's not a bad seat in the house) are often available from individual ticket-holders in a "scalper-free zone" outside the ballpark. Access Orioles info online at http://www.theorioles.com/index.htm.

Hoops 'n' hardwood... In 1978—way back during the Carter administration—the Washington Bullets won the NBA title; it's been downhill ever since. Bizarre draft choices (the Bullets once had seven-foot-six Manute Bol and barely-five-foot "Muggsy" Bogues on the floor at the same time), bad coaching, and general weirdness conspired to produce a hapless team that stayed that way for most of the eighties. But the 1994 acquisition of Chris Webber and Juwan Howard, coupled with seven-foot-seven Romanian center Gheroghe Muresan (who wears uniform number 77), turned the Bullets into a team that actually made the playoffs in the 1996–97 season. In response to criticism that its name, in light of D.C.'s murder rate, was in bad taste, the team officially changed its moniker to the **Washington Wizards** (tel 301/622–3865; http://www.nba.com/wizards) beginning with the 1997–98 season. (Predictably, the new name, too, has drawn criticism for being boring, having nothing to do with Washington, and evoking the Ku Klux Klan). They moved in 1997 into the new MCI Center downtown, and single-game tickets should be available. Washington has a long tradition of big-time college basketball, too, with Georgetown University and the University of Maryland leading the way. The **Georgetown Hoyas** (tel 202/687–4692) play in USAirways Arena and the **Maryland Terrapins** (tel 301/314–7062, Cole Field House, University Blvd. at

Stadium Dr.) compete on the campus in suburban College Park, Maryland.

Slapshots... Thanks to a local sports columnist, the **Washington Capitals** (tel 301/386–7000; http://www.clark.net/pub/southern/capitals/capitals.html) have for years been known by another nickname: the Choking Dogs. Team owner Abe Pollin, who also owns the Wizards, has been criticized for focusing on the basketball team at the Caps' expense. Washington is not a hockey town like Montreal or Boston; the conventional wisdom is that the Caps have exactly 11,000 fans and they all go to every home game. They may get some more, though, with the team's move into MCI Center in the 1997–98 season.

Soccer it to 'em... The first year of Major League Soccer, the pro league begun in response to the World Cup's 1994 success in the U.S., was nowhere more successful than in Washington, where the **D.C. United** (tel 202/333-1880; http://www.clark.net/pub/mmathai/mls/index.html) won the 1997 championship. The level of play is not as high as the premiere English, Italian, or South American leagues, but it is still good, and some of the 1994 World Cup international stars have joined the league. The United plays in RFK Stadium, which they have to themselves now that the Redskins have fled for the burbs. Single-game tickets are easy to get and D.C.'s sizable, soccer-mad Latino population turns RFK into a huge party for home games. There is also a professional indoor soccer team, the **Washington Warthogs** (tel 301/350–3400), who now have USAirways Arena all to themselves. Indoor soccer is a mix of soccer and a video game: The field is a hockey rink with the ice replaced by Astroturf. Warthogs games are full of fan-participation gimmicks, most aimed at kids, and feel more like pop concerts than indoor soccer games—which is not necessarily a bad thing.

A night at the races... Horse racing is illegal in the District of Columbia, but in Maryland you can bet on trifectas to your heart's content. Ponies and their sulkies trot Thursday through Saturday nights at **Rosecroft Raceway** (tel 301/567–4000, 6336 Rosecroft Dr., Fort

Washington, MD), winter or summer; Tuesday nights are added in summer. The raceway also features "simulcast" betting, which makes it possible to bet on races around the country.

Where to play

Eight ball in the side pocket... You can't spit in the District without hitting a funky little pool hall. The most authentically atmospheric is **Atomic Billiards** (tel 202/363–7665, 3427 Connecticut Ave., NW) in Cleveland Park, distinguished by its early-thrift-store decor. There's also **Bedrock Billiards** (tel 202/667–7665, 1841 Columbia Rd., NW) in Adams-Morgan, which has—you guessed it—a Flintstones theme; and trendy **Buffalo Billiards** (tel 202/331–7665, 1330 19th St., NW) in Dupont Circle, the largest of the three, with 30 tables—it's so popular it gives out pagers to those waiting to get in. All keep proper pool hall hours, which is to say good 'n' late: Atomic and Bedrock until 1am Monday through Thursday, 2am Friday and Saturday, midnight Sunday, and Buffalo an hour later than that.

Smooth skating ahead... A winter visit to D.C. has at least two advantages: fewer tourists and more chances to ice-skate. The most picturesque place to cut the ice is the Reflecting Pool in front of the **Lincoln Memorial**, a surface that is unfortunately only available when it's record-breakingly cold. You'll have to bring your own skates to cut the ice here; skate rentals are available at the **National Sculpture Garden Ice Rink** (tel 202/371–5340, 7th St. at Constitution Ave., SE), which is open weekdays until 10pm and weekends until 11, and at the indoor **Bethesda Metro Ice Center** (tel 301/656–0588, Wisconsin Ave. and Old Georgetown Rd., NW), which is an easy trek up Wisconsin Avenue from the District.

Bowling for (tax) dollars... You can't do it in the District unless you live in the White House, where there are private lanes. Since bowling's retro chic has utterly failed to bowl over the locals, don't bother looking for grunge bowling or rock 'n' bowl or even karaoke 'n' bowl nights. If bowl you must, try the **Bowl America** in Maryland (tel

301/585–6990, 8616 Cameron St., Silver Spring, MD), a place that may help you understand why places to bowl are called alleys; it's open until 1am on Friday and Saturday nights. The vast 48-lane **Bowl America** in Falls Church (tel 703/534–1370, 140 S. Maple Ave., Falls Church, VA, open daily until midnight) is clean, well-lighted, and equipped with automatic scoring. If you want to bowl just a little, **Tuffy Leemans Duck Pin Bowling** (tel 301/942–4200, Georgia Ave. at Randolph Rd., Glenmont, MD) is the place: duck pins (a.k.a. candlepins) are smaller than regular bowling pins, as are the balls, and you get three rolls per frame. It's open until 10pm Monday–Friday, until midnight Friday and Saturday nights.

Rollerama... D.C. is as good a place to be a Rollerblader as it is a bad place to be a bowler. The closed-off portion of **Pennsylvania Avenue** directly in front of the White House is ideal for skating into the wee hours. The ugly concrete expanse that is **Freedom Plaza** (13th St. at Pennsylvania Ave., NW) attracts skaters into early evening, and is also a favorite spot for skateboarding. The enormous **Pentagon parking lot**, right off I-95 across the Potomac in Virginia, is frequented by in-line skaters after hours and on weekends. In-line skates can be rented from **City Bikes** (tel 202/265–1564, 2501 Champlain St., NW, open until 7pm most nights, Sunday until 5pm, Thursday until 9pm) and from the **Ski Chalet** (tel 703/521–1700, 2704 Columbia Pike, Arlington, VA, open until 7:30pm Mon–Fri, 5pm weekends). You can reach the **Washington Area Rollerskaters** at 202/466–5005 for further information on skating routes and in-liners events.

Running free... As in any big city, the rule for after-dark jogging in D.C. is simple: Stick to the main drags. The mile-and-a-half-long exercise trail along **Rock Creek Parkway**, which begins at Connecticut Avenue and Calvert Street, NW, draws runners from very early in the morning to very late at night, though exercising alongside four lanes of exhaust-spewing traffic seems counterproductive. Other popular spots for an after-work jog are along the **Tidal Basin**, on the **National Mall** (Bill Clinton's customary morning choice), and, when it's not too crowded, at the **National Zoo** (tel 202/673–4800, 3001 Connecticut Ave., NW), which is open until 8pm during the summer months. The **D.C. Road Runners Club** (tel 703/241–0395) and **Washington Runhers** (get it?) (tel 703/690–2094) can suggest other running routes and tell you about upcoming clinics and races.

Frisbee freebie... All kinds of sports are played on the National Mall (that broad grassy swath between the Capitol and the Washington Monument), everything from volleyball to football to softball to cricket, but foremost among them is Frisbee. There's almost always a pickup game underway, especially during the summer, until the last glimmer of dusk is gone. Look for the No. 1 indication of nearby Frisbee players: dogs wearing bandannas.

Workout arrangements... Washington's health clubs serve the gamut of American yupppiedom, from torture chambers of grunting macho macho men, to Seinfeldish singles scenes, to high-tech palaces for political trophy wives and their over-the-Hill hubbies. Most gyms admit only members or charge mightily for day passes. This cost can often be reduced either by going as the guest of a local who is a member, or by obtaining a free day pass by feigning interest in joining. **Results** (tel 202/518–0001, 1612 U St., NW), a spacious new facility in an old warehouse space, charges nonmembers $15 a day. It's open 6am–11pm Monday–Friday, 8am–10pm Saturday, 8am–9pm Sunday. At the **Washington Sports Club**, which has several locations around the city, the nonmember day-use fee is $20. The downtown club (tel 202/785–4900, 20th St. at M St., NW) is open 6:30am–10pm Monday–Friday, 9am–7pm Saturday; other branches stay open seven days a week, generally 6:30am–11pm weekdays, 8:30am–8:30pm weekends. The **National Capital YMCA** (tel 202/862–9622, 1711 Rhode Island Ave., NW) is free to anyone who belongs any YMCA nationwide. It stays open until 10:30pm Monday–Friday, though it closes earlier on weekends—6:30pm on Saturday, 5:30pm on Sunday.

Taking a dip... Considering the paucity of public pools in the capital city, if you want to swim you might have to book a hotel with a pool—and there aren't many. The business-oriented, Japanese-owned **ANA Hotel** (tel 202/429-2400, 2401 M St., NW), the superswank **Four Seasons** in Georgetown (tel 202/342-0444, 2800 Pennsylvania Ave., NW), the downtown **J.W. Marriott** (tel 202/393-2000, 1331 Pennsylvania Ave., NW), and the **Ritz-Carlton Pentagon City** across the river (tel 703/415-5000, 1250 S. Hayes St., Arlington, VA) all have lap pools. Or check into the quiet **Canterbury Hotel** (tel 202/393-3000, 1733 N St., NW) or **Governor's House Hotel** (tel 202/296-2100, 17th St. and Rhode Island Ave., NW) and you get complimentary access to the pool at the **National Capital YMCA** (see Workout Arrangements above); otherwise, you'll have to belong to a Y in some other city (or befriend one of the Y's members) to get in.

Boating... The **Tidal Basin Boat House** (tel 202/484-0206) rents paddle-boats in which passengers can putt around under pedal-power on the Tidal Basin in front of the Jefferson Memorial until 7pm daily. Goofy but satisfying. Several sightseeing boats leave from the dock in Old Town, Alexandria. The most popular—and, not surprisingly, the cheapest—trips are those offered by the **Potomac Riverboat Company** (tel 703/684-0580), which conducts round-trip tours between Old Town and Georgetown at 7:30 and 9:30pm. The rides are pretty touristy but not a bad way to see the city from the water.

Subpar experiences... Two public 18-hole golf courses in D.C. are cheap and accessible—and, it should be noted, pretty scuzzy. But hey, you can play until 8pm in summer. Reservations are recommended at both the **Rock Creek Park** course (tel 202/882-7332, 16th St. and Rittenhouse Rd., NW) and the **East Potomac Park** golf course in East Potomac Park (tel 202/554-7660, 972 Ohio Dr., NW). The latter is near the site of D.C.'s ugliest public sculpture, "The Awakening," at Hains Point, the hand and knee of a huge figure that seems to digging himself out of the ground where he was deservedly buried. Eighteen holes of golf will run $15–$20 at either course.

Over the net... Like golf, tennis in Washington tends to be a country club sport, but there are public courts at **Rock Creek Park** (tel 202/722–5949, 16th and Kennedy sts., NW; open daily until 10pm) and **East Potomac Park** (tel 202/554–5962, 1090 Ohio Dr., NW; open Monday–Thursday to 11pm, Fri–Sun to 8pm). Rock Creek's courts are Deco-Turf, East Potomac's a choice of clay or hard surfaces; all outdoor courts are lighted for night play. Both require reservations. Court rental will run $5–$15; indoor courts at both locations cost more.

hangi

5

ng out

You've heard of the city that never sleeps? Washington is the city that never relaxes. Go to any local coffee bar and you'll see patrons with a laptop in one hand and coffee in the other jostling for the seat next to the electrical outlet.

Where success is concerned, Washington has different standards from the rest of the country. I recently ate dinner at a downtown restaurant where a couple at an adjacent table spent the entire meal criticizing a mutual friend's lack of drive and ambition. The friend was the Secretary of Defense. (This story is true. The job title has been changed to protect the slacker in question.)

But all those obsessive, workaholic locals are missing one of D.C.'s greatest attributes: loads of free museums (paid for with your tax dollars) and public spaces ripe for lounging. And although most of those museums shutter up tight at night, the public spaces remain gloriously open after dark. In a cityscape so studded with flood-lit monuments and memorials, even the shortest cab ride can stop your heart with views that, corny as it sounds, are just plain breathtaking, and there's nothing to stop you from getting out of the car and strolling right into the postcard view yourself. Despite all the press inches devoted to Washington's high crime rate, wherever nighttime strollers congregate—notably Dupont Circle, Lafayette Square, the western end of the Mall, and along Wisconsin Avenue in Georgetown—there's reassuring safety in numbers. (On the Mall, there are National Park Service personnel on duty at the various monuments until closing time, which is generally midnight.) There are few more quintessentially Washington experiences—except maybe having your car booted—than buying a Ben & Jerry's Peace Pop from a street vendor and lounging at the base of the Jefferson Memorial on a hot summer night.

Shopping, on the other hand—never one of this city's strong suits—is nearly nonexistent at night. (D.C.'s merchants may be the only people in town who see no virtue in logging overtime.) Those dead set on shopping after dark in D.C. had best stand outside the doors of their favorite retail destination and wait to dash in just as the sun sets—otherwise they're out of luck.

The Lowdown

Caffeine scene... Like most of the Milky Way, the District has Starbucks galore, but that doesn't mean you have to go there. The **Pop Stop** (tel 202/328–0880; 1513 17th St., NW; open Sun–Thur to 2am, Fri–Sat to 4am) is one of the few places in town where you can gab over coffee all night long without feeling conspicuous. This two-story town house has splashy Keith Haring–style flowers on the wall, two floors full of crappy old chairs and sofas, and a great vanilla latte. And while you're coffee-bar hopping, sample the pastries at **Jolt N' Bolt** (tel 202/232–0077; 1918 18th St., NW; open Sun–Thur to 11pm, Fri–Sat to midnight) south of Adams-Morgan, which has plenty of living-room-like ambience, despite its frankly utilitarian name. Both the Pop Stop and Jolt N' Bolt offer outdoor seating in summer, a welcome relief while dawdling away those muggy August nights. The less atmospheric but nearly-always-open **Soho Tea & Coffee** (tel 202/463–7646; 2150 P St., NW; open daily to 4am) is home of the city's only coffee happy hour. Situated on one of Dupont Circle's busiest corners, with big storefront windows that make for great people watching, it's frequented by the postclub and the pre-exam crowds. **Liquid** (tel 202/232–4000, 2337 18th St., NW) is a stylish new coffee bar in Adams-Morgan, that rare neighborhood that actually desperately needs a coffee bar. The overdesigned space, in stark silver and white, looks a little like one of Tim Burton's *Batman* snowscapes. It's open daily until 11pm, and also features a juice bar and Internet access, making it the first D.C. restaurant on the "cyber cafe" bandwagon.

A long-overdue alternative in a coffeecentric world, **Teaism** (tel 202/667–3827; 2009 R St., NW; open Sun–Thur to 10pm, Fri–Sat to 11pm) serves more than 30 different kinds of tea, along with Japanese-inspired food like cilantro scrambled eggs and ginger hamburgers. While it's not open quite as late as the coffee bars (tea does deliver somewhat less of a caffeine bang for your buck), there's nothing quite like the Anglophilic satisfaction of being able to order Oolong or Kenya Black tea by the pot. Teaism has gotten so much local attention that evenings and weekends are crowded and there's a staffer stationed upstairs to ward off seating disputes.

Orienteering on the Mall... There's one place in Washington where you can always hang out after dark: the **National Mall,** that 2-mile swath of lawn running east and west from the Capitol to Potomac Park, bounded on the north and south by Constitution and Independence avenues. Here is where the million men marched, where a president gets inaugurated every 4 years, where fireworks fill the evening skies each July 4th. The ornate dome of the **U.S. Capitol,** where the city's four quadrants converge, presides over the easternmost end of the Mall; the Capitol grounds are open all hours to the public, and people frequently stroll around here, particularly in summer and around Christmas (there's after-hours parking on the Independence Avenue side). Look up to see lit windows where Hill staffers toil late, burning the taxpayers' midnight oil. The Mall's approximate center point is the **Washington Monument;** west of there, the Mall is pretty much all monument territory. The **Reflecting Pool** forms an east-west axis between the Washington Monument and the **Lincoln Memorial,** which is flanked by the **Vietnam Veterans Memorial** and the **Korean War Veterans Memorial;** to the south of Washington's obelisk lie the Tidal Basin and the **Jefferson Memorial**. The Mall's eastern half is lined with the Smithsonian museums, with hulking federal office buildings behind them. Exceptions to the humdrum federal architecture here include the **National Gallery of Art**'s white marble East Wing (between 3rd and 4th sts. along Pennsylvania Ave.), with its sharply angled optical-illusion of a facade designed by I.M. Pei; the circular, multistoried **Hirshhorn Museum** (7th St. at Independence Ave.), which is hollow inside and looks a lot like a carburetor; and the **Smithsonian Institution Building** (1000 Jefferson Dr.), a Gothic Revival castle that now houses the remains of Smithsonian founder James Smithson.

In search of dead presidents... The largest and hardest-to-ignore monument in the capital city is, of course, the **Washington Monument** (tel 202/426–6840). You don't need directions to get there; newcomers to the area use it like the North Star to find their way home. (Buildings in the District are forbidden by law to exceed its height.) From April to Labor Day, you can take the elevator to the top any time up until 11:45pm, when the last elevator leaves; the rest of the year the doors close at 5pm. The summer nighttime hours are a boon—the wait to get in is cooler after dark, with lines considerably shorter, and once you get upstairs the nighttime view is more dramatic. Note: repair work may close down the monument for up to three months sometime in 1998, so call ahead. Those who can't resist interpreting the Washington Monument as an oversized phallic symbol should note that the original plan was for something far more ornate, in which the obelisk was only one design element. Lack of both money and public enthusiasm caused the plan to be scaled back until only the obelisk was left. Even so, after construction started in 1848, the project ground to a halt and wasn't finished until 1884, which is why the monument changes color 150 feet up (the original quarry ran out of stone in the interim). These days, it gets more respect: In recent years, a series of safe-sex posters depicting the monument wearing a giant condom was quickly squashed due to public outcry.

One can only imagine what the same campaign would have done to the domed rotunda of the **Jefferson Memorial** (tel 202/426–6822), set picturesquely on the south bank of the Tidal Basin. Nineteenth-century detractors called the structure "Jefferson's Muffin," but the basement display (open until midnight) of rejected designs for the monument provides plenty of evidence that we got off easy, eyesore-wise. Being so close to the water makes this monument a great place to loll on summer evenings; in late March or early April, when the Japanese cherry trees that line the Tidal Basin are in full bloom, late evenings are about the only time to visit without risking cherry-blossom gridlock. In 1974, Ways and Means Committee Chairman Wilbur Mills was pulled over near the Tidal Basin while driving with stripper

Fanne Foxe and another woman; in the ensuing fracas, Foxe earned her place in history by jumping in. Mills resigned his post not long thereafter; Foxe subsequently billed herself as "The Tidal Basin Stripper."

At the far end of the Mall, directly west of the Washington Monument, the **Lincoln Memorial** (tel 202/426–6895) has always provided a backdrop for causes and controversy: Here Marian Anderson sang on Easter 1939 after being barred from the D.A.R.'s Constitution Hall because she was black; here Martin Luther King delivered his "I Have a Dream" speech in August 1963. Protesters and mourners of all kinds still gather on its steps, most recently in 1996 for a candlelight vigil the day after Jerry Garcia died.

Nighttime browsers at once gravitated to the mall's newest monument, opened in 1997: the **Franklin Delano Roosevelt Memorial,** set on the strip of land between the Tidal Basin and the Potomac, fairly equidistant between the Jefferson and Lincoln memorials. Designed by a landscape architect, it consists of a series of outdoor "rooms" that contain inscriptions of the president's words, symbolic waterfalls, and a statue of beloved Eleanor Roosevelt—the first presidential monument that has included a first lady in its depiction. When the monument opened, there was considerable controversy about the fact that Roosevelt was nowhere shown in his wheelchair; President Clinton has decreed that this politically incorrect oversight should be remedied, but at press time the details were still being worked out in Congress (don't hold your breath).

Sights you won't see from your tour bus... Where do Washingtonians go for first-class entertainment? The Kennedy Center? The National? Heck no, they bring lawn chairs, coolers, and portable stereos to the highway turnoff at the north end of the **National Airport runway** to watch planes take off. It's a crowd scene on hot summer nights, with families, college kids, and ironists planting themselves in the flight path for hours. Take George Washington Memorial Highway south toward the airport, but take the Gravely Point left exit before you get there.

Behind the M Street Exxon station at the base of the Key Bridge are the so-called ***Exorcist* steps**—the steep staircase down which two characters in the 1973 horror hit *The Exorcist* fell to their death, having been pitched out of Linda Blair's bedroom window by Satan. At night, lit by a streetlight, it still looks haunting, just like the image from the movie poster. If you're driving around the neighborhood at night, swing past the modest row house (still a private home) at **1212 T Street, NW,** where Duke Ellington grew up—he lived there until he turned 21 and left for New York with his band, the Washingtonians.

Another offbeat drive-by sight is **St. Elizabeths Hospital** (2700 Martin Luther King Ave., SE), known as the U.S. Government Insane Asylum until the Civil War, which has had its share of well-known tenants. Poet Ezra Pound was incarcerated in St. Es from 1946 until 1958 after he was declared unfit to stand trial for treason. The hospital's most infamous contemporary tenant is John Hinckley, who attempted to endear himself to Jodie Foster in 1981 by shooting President Reagan.

War stories... Though controversial at the outset, the **Vietnam Veterans Memorial** (northeast of the Lincoln Memorial, in Constitution Gardens between 21st and 22nd sts., NW) nowadays attracts more visitors than any other monument in the city. Popularly known as "The Wall," Maya Lin's subtle design—a black marble V sunk into the earth and inscribed with the names of the dead and missing—is strikingly sober and dignified, and undeniably moving. It's just as popular a hangout at night as it is in the daytime. Thick books with plastic-covered pages list the inscribed names and their locations on the wall. People leave so many mementos here that they have become a sort of monument unto themselves (though periodically removed by the Park Service, many are included in the Museum of American History's "Personal Legacy" exhibit).

Opened in 1995, the **Korean War Veterans Memorial** (just southeast of the Lincoln Memorial) depicts 19 larger-than-life infantrymen on the march. At night, the soldiers are eerily lifelike. On the northern border of Arlington Cemetery, just off U.S. Route 50, is the **Marine Corps War Memorial,** better known as "Iwo Jima" because it's based on AP photographer Joseph Rosenthal's famous shot of marines planting the American flag on Iwo Jima island. Although most Washingtonians appreciate its charms as a drive-by sight, the memorial also gained notoriety during the '70s as a gay cruising spot, a use which has dwindled since then.

Neighborhoods to stroll... The neighborhood that best approximates what is generally meant by "street life" is **Georgetown.** Crammed with restaurants and bars, Georgetown's M Street and Wisconsin Avenue have a high volume of nighttime foot traffic, and as a result their stores are open late—which in D.C. usually means until 9pm—while restaurants and bars buzz on into the wee, wee hours. The down side is that it's not easily accessible by Metro, parking is a bitch, and the sidewalks are thronged with people you think you may have seen at that frat party you ditched back in the early eighties. The residential sector of Georgetown is well worth a walk, though, and not just the one you'll take to and from your car. Residential areas start a block off of the main Wisconsin Avenue drag; you could walk to Georgetown from Dupont Circle via P Street, or walk across Prospect Street to Georgetown University at 37th and Prospect streets. Many of Georgetown's playhouse-scale—and, today, astronomically expensive—homes pre-date the founding of Washington.

Locals, however, will be in the area surrounding **Dupont Circle,** whose attractions include a mix of restaurants, bars, clubs, bookstores, and movie theaters. Nocturnal types even hang out in the circle itself, a grassy common ringed with benches and crisscrossed with walkways; regulars play chess in the evenings at the built-in tables on the northeast side. In the middle of the circle is a large ornamental fountain (unlit at night, unfortunately—it's District-maintained) sculpted by Daniel Chester French, better known for designing the Lincoln Memorial's presidential statuary. If you don't mind sharing your space with bullying pigeons, 90-mile-per-hour Rollerbladers, and muttering men wearing four overcoats, there are worse places to spend a summer evening. A short walk northwest up Massachusetts Avenue toward Sheridan Circle takes you to an area dubbed Embassy Row, where several elaborate 19th-century mansions, their foreign flags and seals floodlit at night, run the diplomatic affairs of their respective countries. (That's the high-rent Embassy Row; the legations of more troubled nations like Nicaragua, Namibia, and Rwanda are quartered on the less show-offy New Hampshire Avenue, northeast of Dupont Circle.)

The Mall excepted, **Old Town Alexandria** has the area's highest concentration of tourists; the 20-minute drive (40 minutes by subway) to Old Town makes visiting here a snap. In addition to nautical-themed bars and restaurants, King Street, the main drag, has zillions of gift shops selling doilies and bath salts, as well as tour guides walking around in full colonial garb, even in the evenings. In addition to such kitsch, however, the out-of-towners attract a wide variety of street performers and musicians, which you won't find anywhere else. It's possible to enjoy Old Town without actually going indoors; King Street dead-ends at the water, where riverfront benches and a pier are open to the public.

Vistas... When Washingtonians hear "vista," they generally think of the downtown hotel where Mayor Marion Barry was busted for using crack cocaine. (It's still there, by the way, though it's called the ANA now.) If what you're after, though, is a more literal perspective, many consider that the best view of the city is from the parking lot at the **Our Lady of Perpetual Help** church (tel 202/678–4999, 1600 Morris Rd., SE) in Anacostia—but it's not a safe place to go at night. There's always the top of the **Washington Monument,** of course, which stays open until midnight April through August; if repair work has shut things down, or if you run into a line there, which is possible during peak tourist season, try instead the 315-foot-high **Old Post Office Observatory** (tel 202/606–8691; 1100 Pennsylvania Ave., NW; open to 11pm mid-April through mid-September) for a lookout that rivals the Washington Monument's. Picking your way around the great gears of the tower's clock can be fun, and the tourist shops of the Old Post Office Pavilion below stay open until 9pm. From May through October, another option is the open-air Roof Top Terrace at the **Hotel Washington** (tel 202/638–5900, 515 15th St., NW, open until 1am Mon–Sat, midnight on Sun). For the price of a drink, you can enjoy a spectacular, sparkling view of nighttime Washington. For a drive-by panorama, one of the highest geographic points in the city is on 13th Street at Clifton Terrace; to the south, the breadth of the city suddenly appears before you.

Palm readers... Despite—or perhaps because of—being a facts-and-figures kind of place, Washington has quite a number of palmists, with new ones popping up in dusty, red-curtained storefronts every day. In Dupont Circle, there's **The Mystic Place** (tel 202/483–8370, 1728 Connecticut Ave., NW), and in Georgetown, **Mrs. Natalie of Georgetown** (tel 202/333–1245, 1259 Wisconsin Ave., NW). Drop-in customers are welcome; both stay open until 8pm or so, and the cost of a 20- to 30-minute session is $5–$15, depending on what services you require (both read tarot cards as well as palms).

Window shopping... Three of D.C.'s Maryland suburbs—Chevy Chase, Bethesda, and Potomac—recently appeared on a U.S. Census study of the 10 zip codes in the country with the highest per-capita number of millionaires. Which goes a long way toward explaining why the city's best window shopping is just over the Maryland border in Chevy Chase, where a two-block stretch of Wisconsin Avenue is a dead ringer for Rodeo Drive. Staying open late would be déclassé, of course, but the display windows are well worth a gawk at night. This is where you'll find **Cartier** (tel 301/654–5858, 5454 Wisconsin Ave.) and **Tiffany's** (tel 301/657–8777, 5500 Wisconsin Ave.), **Saks Fifth Avenue** (tel 301/657–9000, 5555 Wisconsin Ave.) and **Gianni Versace** (tel 301/907–9400, 5454 Wisconsin Ave.), to name just a few. And if you're hanging out in Cleveland Park, perhaps after a meal at the Yenching Palace (see Late Night Dining), get a kick out of the windows of **Wake Up Little Susie** (tel 202/244–0700, 3409 Connecticut Ave., NW), the place to go for handmade jewelry and ceramics, wall clocks shaped like fruit, and pop-culture phenomena like the Magnetic Poetry Kit.

The mesmerizing window displays at **Mobili** (tel 202/337–2100, 2201 Wisconsin Ave., NW) are not to be missed if you're night-owling on the upper Georgetown strip along Wisconsin Avenue—the ultramodern Italian furniture here often looks like it was designed by Dr. Seuss, and that's meant as a compliment. If you have some time to kill in Adams-Morgan—while waiting for a table at Cities, perhaps (see Late Night Dining and The Club Scene)—check out the creatures scaling the building's facade at **Skynear & Co.** (tel 202/797–7160, 1800 Wyoming Ave., NW), a flamboyant furniture store along

Adams-Morgan's 18th Street main drag. Peek inside at the purple velvet couches and wall sconces shaped like gargoyles. Then take in the window displays at **Retrospective** (tel 202/483–8112, 2324 18th St., NW), a vintage-home-furnishings shop with some stunning chrome appliances; nearby **Shake Your Booty** (tel 202/518–8205, 2335 18th St., NW), which offers outlandish footwear like platform tennis shoes and zebra-skin boots; and **Rerun** (tel 202/319–2125, 2475 18th St., NW), which has an intriguing selection of thrift-shop clothing from the seventies. And speaking of vintage furnishings, U Street's two-story **Millennium** (tel 202/483–1218, 1528 U St., NW) specializes in "classic mid-century design for the home'—it's a sort of mini-mall for Eisenhower-era furniture and housewares—and it's even open until 8pm on weekends, just right for pre-club browsing.

Late-night browsing in Georgetown... Few stores in the Washington area keep late-night hours; the exceptions are mostly in Georgetown, where the nighttime tourist traffic makes staying open late (we're talking 9pm here) a good bet for merchants. The ubiquitous **Urban Outfitters** (tel 202/342–1012, 3111 M St., NW) features pricey faux-retro gear for middle-class teenagers and grown-ups who should know better. **Bootlegger** (tel 202/333–0373, 1420 Wisconsin Ave., NW) and **Commander Salamander** (tel 202/333–9599, 1420 Wisconsin Ave., NW), which share a storefront, sell funky shoes and somewhat dated punk regalia, respectively. And though its notorious groupie-chick look is now outré, **Betsey Johnson** (tel 202/338-4090, 1319 Wisconsin Ave., NW) is still the place to go for a Spandex tube dress.

Gourmet to go... Forget the Safeway—Washington is prime territory for snob-appeal groceries, and the most lavish and extravagant of them all is Georgetown's **Dean and Deluca** (tel 202/342–2500, 1027 Connecticut Ave., NW), which betrays its Manhattan roots by staying open until 9pm Friday and Saturday (8pm other nights). In this rambling brick building you can buy high-end foodstuffs like mesclun, quail eggs, kumquats, and imported lemon curd; the meat window alone is easily as fascinating as most of the city's art galleries. In Cleveland Park, **Vace Italian**

Delicatessen (tel 202/363–1999; 3315 Connecticut Ave., NW; open daily until 9 pm) has imported olives and cheeses, fresh pastas and sauces, and, of course, take-out pizza. In Dupont Circle, **Sutton on the Run** (tel 202/588–9876; R St. at Connecticut Ave., NW; open Mon–Sat to 10pm) is the perfect place to get upscale prepared food or imported chocolate—or simply to marvel at how much you just spent on snacks to have in your hotel room. In the same neighborhood, **Market Day** (tel 202/387–3858; 1727 Connecticut Ave., NW; open daily to 10pm) is a gourmet grocery with a large sandwich menu and upstairs seating.

Night galleries... Unlike in some major cities, where evening hours make museums date-worthy venues, Washington's museums generally punch a federal-office-worker clock: Come 5:30pm, they close their doors faster than you can say "three-day weekend." Among the few exceptions is the nonfederal **Corcoran Museum of Art** (tel 202/639–1700, 500 17th St., NW), which stays open until 9 on Thursday nights. The Corcoran's intelligent collection is heavy on American art, ranging from Winslow Homer to Roy Lichtenstein. The gallery is perhaps best known for refusing to house a touring Robert Mapplethorpe exhibit in 1988. The **Library of Congress** (tel 202/707–8000) keeps open the exhibits at its Madison Building Gallery (1st St. at Independence Ave.) until 9:30 Monday through Friday. The Exhibition Hall at the **National Archives** (tel 202/501–5000, 7th St. at Constitution Ave., NW), where you can stare wonderingly at originals of the Magna Carta, Constitution, and Bill of Rights, stays open until 9pm year-round. Between June 14 and Labor Day, three of the Mall's Smithsonian museums—the **National Air and Space Museum,** the **National Museum of American History,** and the **National Museum of Natural History**—extend their usual hours all the way to 6:30pm. That extra hour might be just enough to let you dash into Air and Space and see the *Spirit of St. Louis,* to peek into American History at the remains of the flag that inspired the national anthem, and to glimpse, for a risky second, the Hope Diamond at Natural History.

Walk and talk and squawk with the animals... The **National Zoological Park** (tel 202/673–4800, 3001 Connecticut Ave., NW) is open until 8pm from May 1 to September 15, or at least the outside enclosures are (buildings close at 6pm). The zoo, which started out as a conglomeration of animal pens outside the Smithsonian Castle on the Mall (the Smithsonian's taxidermists needed live models to work from), moved in 1890 to its current location. The zoo's grounds were laid out by Frederick Law Olmsted, who also designed New York's Central Park—hence the name of its main thoroughfare, Olmsted Walk. These days the zoo is renowned for its conservation efforts, its biggest success to date being the goofy-looking long-tailed South American marmoset, the golden lion tamarin. Its best-known resident is Hsing-Hsing, the surviving giant panda given to President Nixon by China in 1972. (His mate, Ling-Ling, died in 1992; Hsing-Hsing himself underwent successful surgery for testicular cancer in the spring of 1997.) The most popular residents, however, are the youngest: Locals pack the place to see the pair of rhinos and the gorilla born in fall 1996 and spring 1997, respectively. Gardeners should note that the zoo sells what may be D.C.'s best souvenir: exotic manure called "Zoo Doo," culled from the cages of its herbivores.

Tattoo you... Washington might seem like the kind of place where the demand for tattoos hovers somewhere around zero. Not so. At Georgetown's **Jinx Proof** (tel 202/337–JINX, 3306 M St., NW, open daily until 10pm), where the showroom is literally covered in tattoo designs and the low hum of the electric needle is audible in the background, they even take ATM cards. If you're one of those people who just likes to watch, people being tattooed are visible, but from a distance. The print ads for **The Great Southern Tattoo Co.** (tel 301/474–8820, 9403 Baltimore Blvd., College Park, MD, open Tues–Sun until 9pm) stipulate that sobriety is "a must." For customers of less vigilant establishments, there's the **Cosmetic Laser Clinic** (tel 301/897–8844, 5632 Shields Dr., Bethesda, MD; occasional evening hours, call for times), which specializes in laser tattoo removal.

Body piercing: The hole story... In the ever-evolving realm of body modification, tattooing now seems almost quaint. Which explains why **Jinx Proof** (see Tattoo You, above) also does piercing. The price varies by body part, but a navel, for instance, will run you about $30. **The Leather Rack** (tel 202/797–7401, 1723 Connecticut Ave., NW, open until 11pm), which carries body jewelry as well as leather goods, will pierce your nipple and sell you a ring to put in it. And **Perforations** (tel 202/289–8863, 900 M St., NW, open until 8 weeknights, 9pm weekends) does both piercing and branding.

X-rated stuff... It is one of Washington's many ironies that, while you can't get a decent bagel, there are plenty of places to pick up patent-leather thigh-high boots and a 13-inch dildo. Go figure. **The Pleasure Place** (in Georgetown at tel 202/333–8570, 1063 Wisconsin Ave., NW; and near Dupont Circle, tel 202/483–3297, 1710 Connecticut Ave., NW), "Washington's premiere erotic boutique," has it all: edible panties, fishnet stockings, flavored lubricants, and inflatable sex partners (including a sheep-shaped model called "The Embraceable Ewe"). Both branches are open until midnight Wednesday–Saturday, 7pm on Sunday and 10pm Monday and Tuesday. For apparel there's **Dream Dresser** (in Georgetown at tel 202/625–0373, 1042 Wisconsin Ave., NW, open Mon–Sat until 8pm), which carries dominatrix garb and a gruesome array of "dungeon apparatus." The goods these shops carry seem destined for in-home use; although hookers can generally be seen waiting for business in the vicinity of McPherson Square or Thomas Circle, there's no out-and-out porno district. Washington's too discreet for that.

By the book... One question arises from the culture of complaint surrounding Washington's dearth of cutting-edge nightlife: What's everybody doing instead? The answer, of course, is reading, or at least wandering around bookstores looking for books. As in most cities, bookstores here are among the shops that keep the latest hours (often until 9pm or so), so if you've just gotta check whether you're named in the latest White House tell-all memoir, you can do it after committee hearings have wound down for the day. Dominating the scene are two megastores, both of which have in-store cafes: Two-story **Borders Books and Records** (tel 202/466–4999; 1801

K St., NW; open Mon–Fri to 10 pm, Sat to 9pm) downtown and three-story **Barnes & Noble** (202/965–9880; 3040 M St., NW; open daily to 11pm) in Georgetown. The cafe scene is even more pivotal for **Kramerbooks** (tel 202/387–1400; 1517 Connecticut Ave., NW; open Sun–Thur to 1am, Fri–Sat 24 hours). It does have a respectable multipurpose selection, but the books are mostly a backdrop for the adjacent restaurant and bar, Afterwords (see Late Night Dining). Downtown's **Chapters** (tel 202/347–5495, 1512 K St., NW), probably the city's best-loved literary bookstore, holds frequent evening readings after its 6:30pm closing time; schedules are available at the store. **Olsson's Books and Records** (tel 202/785–2664; 1307 19th St., NW; open Mon–Sat to 10pm, Sun to 7pm; and tel 202/338–9544; 1239 Wisconsin Ave., NW; open Mon–Thur to 11pm, Fri–Sat to midnight, Sun to 10pm), a local chain, is a bit pricey—especially its CDs—but it carries a well-rounded stock of best-sellers, classic fiction, and so on.

There are specialty bookstores to suit every taste. The gay community drops by **Lambda Rising** (tel 202/462–6969; 1525 Connecticut Ave., NW; open daily to midnight), which has a comprehensive selection of gay-interest books, as well as **Lammas Women's Books and More** (tel 202/775–8218; 1426 21st St., NW; open Mon–Fri to 10pm, Fri–Sat to midnight, Sun to 8pm), which carries feminist and lesbian literature. Along the Connecticut Avenue strip, nightbirds can alight at the **Politics & Prose Bookstore and Cafe** (tel 202/364–1919; 5015 Connecticut Ave., NW; open Sun–Thur to 10:30pm, Fri–Sat to midnight) for just what the name says—the sort of printed matter that Washingtonians live for. There's always a literate crowd of browsers poring over the used books at the rambling **Second Story Books** (tel 202/659–8884; 2000 P St., NW; open daily to 10pm) in Dupont Circle, or hunting for a secondhand find at **Idle Times** (tel 202/232–4774; 2410 18th St., NW; open daily to 10pm) in Adams-Morgan.

A sacred sight... The **Washington National Cathedral** (tel 202/537–6200, Massachusetts Ave. at Wisconsin Ave., NW) is the sixth largest cathedral in the world, and despite its Gothic lineaments it's thoroughly modern—it enshrines a piece of moon rock and features briefcase-carrying gargoyles. The building itself remains open until 9pm on weekdays between May and August, but the grounds are always open, including the Bishop's Garden, where it's hard to go at night without interrupting a necking couple. It's safe to walk around the grounds even after 11pm.

Flower power... The **National Arboretum** (tel 202/245–4521, 3501 New York Ave., NE), a 400-plus-acre park established by Congress in 1927 as a botanical research facility, closes at 5pm, but it gives guided full-moon hikes once a month. They are free, but reservations are required. The arboretum is well worth a visit—who knew the U.S. had a National Herb Garden, much less a National Bonsai Collection? And from late April to late May, the park's 70,000 azaleas are in bloom.

Need a bouquet at the last minute? Try **Dupont Flowers** (tel 202/797–7600, 1900 Q St., NW) in Dupont Circle or **Little Shop of Flowers** (tel 202/387–7255, 1812 Adams Mill Rd., NW) in Adams-Morgan. Of course, if you happen to be dining in Adams-Morgan, both of which stay open into the early evening, the flowers will come to you: The area's ubiquitous long-stemmed-rose vendors march right up to tables and impugn a man's character if he refuses to fork over $5 for a rose for his date.

Newsstands... In Dupont Circle, **The Newsroom** (tel 202/332–1489; 1753 Connecticut Ave., NW; open daily 7am to 9pm) has the city's widest selection of periodicals and daily newspapers from all over the world; it's a handy stop-off for Embassy Row's junior diplomats hungry for the word from home. If you need, say, a copy of today's New Orleans *Times-Picayune* or the latest edition of *Paris Match,* this is the place to go. Browsers welcome.

The other kind of malls... Georgetown Park (3222 M St., NW; open Mon–Sat to 9 pm, Sun to 6 pm) is a mock-old-fashioned exposed-brick-and-brass mall at the edge of the C & O Canal in Georgetown. Shoppers come for the high-end retail, like Godiva Chocolatier and J. Crew; everybody else comes because parking in the underground garage is easier than looking for a space on the street. On upper Wisconsin Avenue where the District meets

Maryland, **Mazza Gallerie** (5300 Wisconsin Ave., NW) and, across the street, the **Chevy Chase Pavilion** (5335 Wisconsin Ave., NW) are similarly high end; both are open until 8pm Monday–Friday, until 6pm Saturday and 5pm Sunday. If what you're after is a full-scale Banana Republic/Victoria's Secret/Crown Books–type shopping mall, the closest one to the city is **Pentagon City** (1100 S. Hayes St., Arlington VA; open Mon–Sat to 9:30pm, Sun to 6pm), which merits its own stop on the Metro's blue and yellow lines.

For the record... Record stores make natural nocturnal hangouts for certain types; in D.C., this may in fact be the best way to find these often-overlooked subcultures. The **Tower Records** (tel 202/331–2400, 2000 Pennsylvania Ave., NW) near George Washington University is open the latest—until midnight daily. Like other big-city Towers, it stocks a huge volume of mostly mainstream music. Sidle up to the "song-finder," an ATM-like machine with a touch-sensitive screen, to match artists with songs and albums—for example, type the word "turtle" and get a comprehensive listing of songs with the word *turtle* in the title, who sang them, and what album they appeared on. Hours of mindless fun. There's a better selection of music by indie acts at small stores like **Flying Saucer Discs** (tel 202/265–3472; 2318 18th St., NW; open Mon–Sat to 9pm, Sun to 6pm) in the District and **Phantasmagoria** (tel 301/949–8886; 11319 Elkin St., Wheaton, MD; open Thur–Tue to 8 pm, closed Wed) in Maryland. And if it's vinyl you're after, try **Joe's Record Paradise** (tel 301/460–8394; 13822 Georgia Ave., Silver Spring, MD; open Mon–Sat to 9pm, Sun to 6pm).

White House antics... The **White House** (1600 Pennsylvania Ave., as if you didn't know) is much prettier by night than by day; the executive mansion is a popular destination for after-hours strollers, who pause along Pennsylvania Avenue to peer through the iron palings to see who's blown 50 grand to sleep in the Lincoln bedroom. The constant presence of guards and Secret Service guys makes this one of D.C.'s safest spots after dark.

late nigh

6

t dining

When Washingtonians eat out, it's generally because Mr. and Mrs. Policy Wonk were both working late on a deadline project and he just made it to the day-care center before it closed while she had to shoot crosstown to get the car at the shop ("God, I don't feel like cooking again—do you want Thai or tapas or Ethiopian?"). Cruising around looking for a place to have waffles after an all-night rave just isn't high on their list of priorities.

So maybe they don't mind that Washington offers so few late-night dining options—surprisingly few for a city of this size and sophistication. Oh, some restaurants go nuts on weekends and stay open until 11 or midnight, but wait too late and you won't even be able to order a pizza. It's a chicken-and-egg situation: Are late-night joints scarce because no one dines late, or do folks not eat out late because there's nothing good open? Who can tell? In this chapter, we list just about everything in town that stays open past 11pm on weekends. All are worth recommending; if the food's not remarkable, something else compensates—music, drinks, desserts, or the buzz of a lively crowd.

Washington does have a high percentage of nice restaurants, of course. By "nice," I mean the sort of restaurants to which one may take visiting heads of state if one is the President of the United States. This expense-account economy favors an early scene, however; many of the top places in town scoot customers out the door by 10 or 10:30pm. And it keeps everyone's prices steep—with the exceptions of New York City, Philadelphia, and San Francisco, it costs more to eat out in Washington than it does in any other city in the U.S. The average per-person cost of a meal in the District was estimated by Zagat's 1996 survey of area restaurants at $24.49, a figure that may strike out-of-towners as high, but that strikes locals as low. I'm not saying I've never eaten out for this amount. I have—at Popeye's.

On the other hand, D.C.'s immigrant population keeps the dining options diverse. Washington has an extraordinary concentration of ethnic restaurants. Chances are there's a restaurant here that caters to your exotic tastes, be they Salvadorean, Vietnamese, Malaysian, Ethiopian, or Azerbaijani. This is a city of gastronomic contradictions: You can order take-out *yum talay* but you can't get a decent egg cream. But unlike in other cities, D.C.'s immigrant restaurateurs close early, often by 10pm; many popular Vietnamese spots are shut up by 8.

If you want to eat out, but are prevented from doing so by agoraphobia or the inability to find a parking space, **A la Carte Express** (tel 202/232–8646) delivers food from a wide range of area restaurants.

Adams-Morgan and Dupont Circle Dining

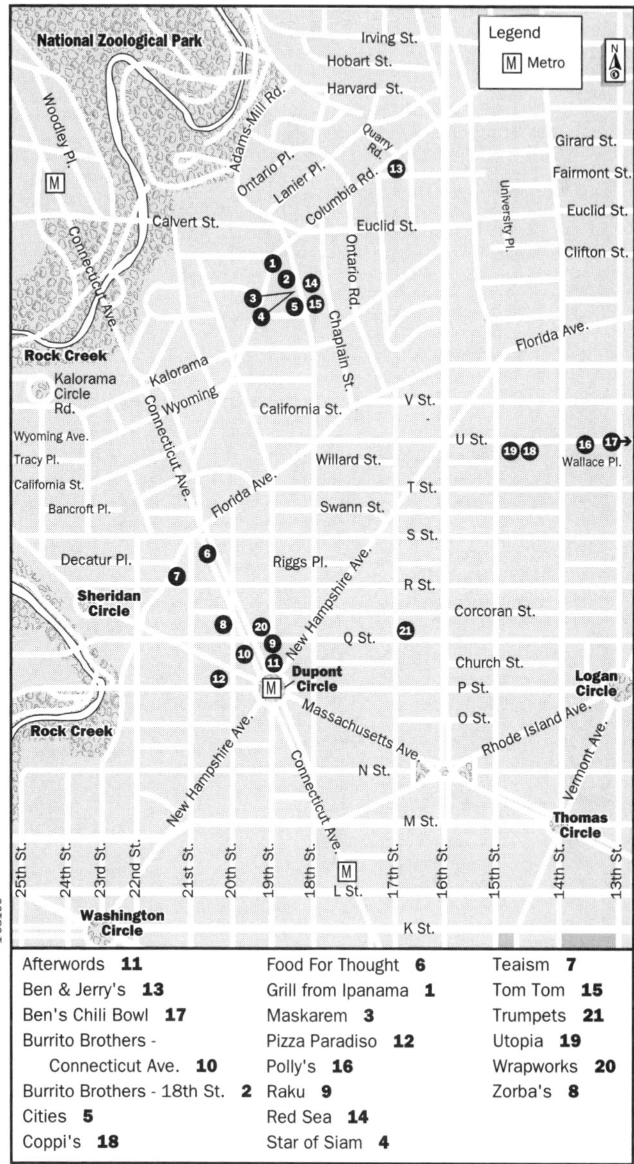

Afterwords **11**
Ben & Jerry's **13**
Ben's Chili Bowl **17**
Burrito Brothers - Connecticut Ave. **10**
Burrito Brothers - 18th St. **2**
Cities **5**
Coppi's **18**
Food For Thought **6**
Grill from Ipanama **1**
Maskarem **3**
Pizza Paradiso **12**
Polly's **16**
Raku **9**
Red Sea **14**
Star of Siam **4**
Teaism **7**
Tom Tom **15**
Trumpets **21**
Utopia **19**
Wrapworks **20**
Zorba's **8**

Georgetown & Downtown Dining

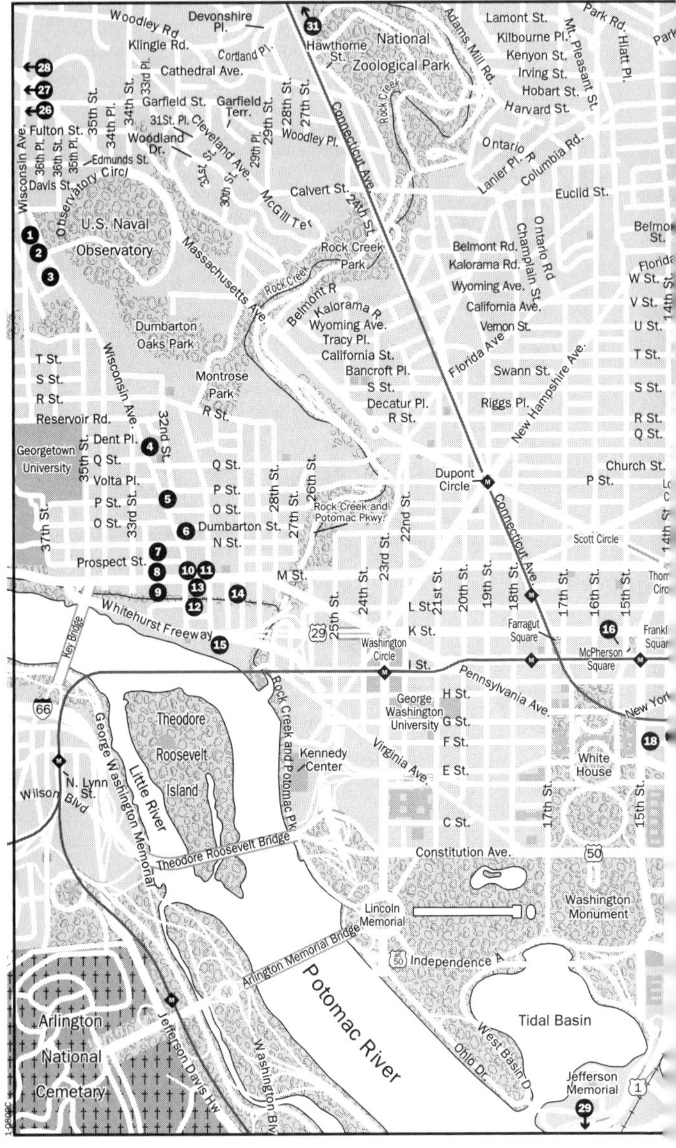

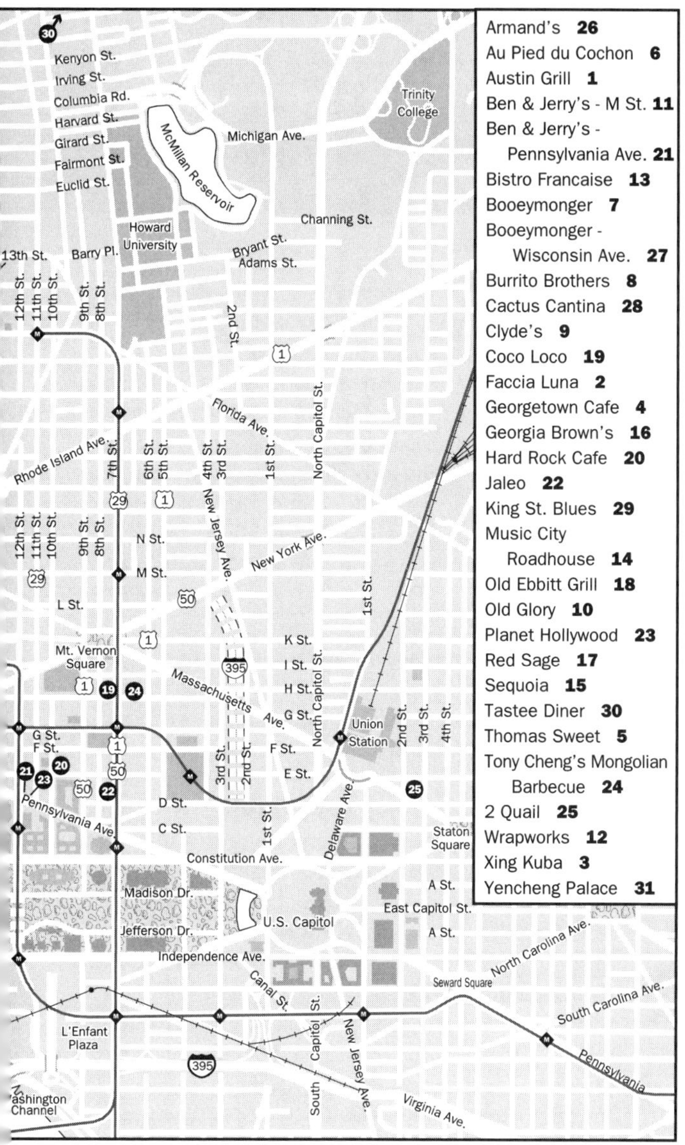
Armand's 26
Au Pied du Cochon 6
Austin Grill 1
Ben & Jerry's - M St. 11
Ben & Jerry's - Pennsylvania Ave. 21
Bistro Francaise 13
Booeymonger 7
Booeymonger - Wisconsin Ave. 27
Burrito Brothers 8
Cactus Cantina 28
Clyde's 9
Coco Loco 19
Faccia Luna 2
Georgetown Cafe 4
Georgia Brown's 16
Hard Rock Cafe 20
Jaleo 22
King St. Blues 29
Music City Roadhouse 14
Old Ebbitt Grill 18
Old Glory 10
Planet Hollywood 23
Red Sage 17
Sequoia 15
Tastee Diner 30
Thomas Sweet 5
Tony Cheng's Mongolian Barbecue 24
2 Quail 25
Wrapworks 12
Xing Kuba 3
Yencheng Palace 31
Kenyon St.
Irving St.
Columbia Rd.
Harvard St.
Girard St.
Fairmont St.
Euclid St.
McMillan Reservoir
Michigan Ave.
Trinity College
Channing St.
Howard University
Barry Pl.
13th St.
Bryant St.
Adams St.
12th St.
11th St.
10th St.
9th St.
8th St.
2nd St.
Florida Ave.
North Capitol St.
Rhode Island Ave.
7th St.
6th St.
5th St.
4th St.
3rd St.
1st St.
New Jersey Ave.
N St.
M St.
L St.
New York Ave.
K St.
Mt. Vernon Square
I St.
H St.
G St.
Massachusetts Ave.
Union Station
F St.
E St.
D St.
C St.
Pennsylvania Ave.
Delaware Ave.
Constitution Ave.
Stanton Square
Madison Dr.
Jefferson Dr.
U.S. Capitol
A St.
East Capitol St.
Independence Ave.
Canal St.
North Carolina Ave.
Seward Square
South Carolina Ave.
L'Enfant Plaza
South Capitol St.
Virginia Ave.
Pennsylvania
Washington Channel

The Lowdown

Tourist traps... Like every city in the world except Baghdad—and it's only a matter of time until that one opens—Washington has a **Hard Rock Cafe.** And, as they do in every other city in the world, tourists line up around the block to get in. The D.C. version features the requisite burger fare and rock memorabilia; its location—down the block from Ford's Theater and across the street from the FBI—guarantees maximum tourist density in the summertime. Close by is **Planet Hollywood,** theme restaurant and tax shelter for Arnold Schwarzenegger, Bruce Willis, et al. Planet Hollywood is decorated with movie-biz memorabilia—the death star model from *Star Wars* sits in the front foyer—and features numerous video screens that allow patrons to watch, for instance, a montage of slo-mo scenes from boxing movies while eating overpriced Denny's-caliber food.

And now for something completely different... Glover Park's tastefully handsome **Xing Kuba** was once the site of the city's best Thai restaurant, Ploy, and we're still sulking about it. Nonetheless, one is forced to admit that Xing Kuba's improbable melange of Asian, New Mexican, and Cuban food is classy and very good. And talk about a gimmick—**Cities** periodically closes and reopens, each time having adopted the decor and cuisine of a different metropolis (until recently Hong Kong, currently Istanbul). The theme doesn't pervade the menu as much as one might hope—adding Turkish coffee to the menu isn't my idea of introducing diners to a new cuisine—but the fact that the food is only passable is irrelevant: It's the scene that's paramount. This restaurant/nightclub is a favorite of the see-and-be-seen crowd, perhaps because of its massive bar (see The Club Scene), which opens onto 18th

Street. Love it or hate it, it's the focal point of Adams-Morgan nightlife.

Places that will impress your date... It bills itself as "Washington's most romantic restaurant," and it might be just that. **2 Quail** is impossibly cozy. Many commentators have faulted this Capitol Hill town house's Laura Ashley-esque decor, but that isn't quite fair; its clutter suggests more Laura Ashley's pack-rat sister. Patrons enjoy the elegant American cuisine—the daily specials are especially good—in big armchairs drawn up to tables in three adjoining rooms crowded with bric-a-brac and garage-sale art. Ask for one of the tables in the niche at the back of the furthermost room. For sheer showmanship, there's **Red Sage,** whose trendy Southwestern decor and cuisine combine to create a grand sense of occasion. The food is out-of-this-world, knock-you-to-your-knees good; the beef tenderloin could convert a vegetarian. It may be a little past its heyday by now, but snag a table by the tree-trunk fireplace and things should heat up nicely for you. But if you adhere to the general principle that anywhere (with the exception of pancake houses) is romantic if you go there late enough, **Bistro Française** in Georgetown is your spot. Open until 3am even on weeknights, it's a striking contrast to the other dining options available at that hour (it has cloth napkins, nonplastic cutlery, etc.) and the French bistro menu sure beats burgers.

Open all night... Georgetown's **Au Pied du Cochon** features a huge mural of a struggling pig about to have its leg hacked off by a smirking butcher. This unfortunate flourish aside, it's a popular on-the-way-home stop for students at nearby Georgetown University and denizens of the neighborhood's trendy nightspots. Look for the small plaque on the red leather banquette marking the spot from which KGB defector Vitaly Yurchenko escaped his captors in 1985. (Legend holds that one of the reasons he gave for re-defecting was that CIA agents forced him to eat the crummy French food at Au Pied.) Down the street is the **Georgetown Cafe,** a nighttime pit stop of last resort where harsh lighting will accent the bags under your eyes nicely. This is not the place to go menu surfing: Stick with scrambled eggs, bacon, and toast. The Washington area is overrun with faux diners, but the two 24-hour **Tastee Diners,** both in Maryland about 20 minutes out of the District, are the real thing. This, of course, has drawbacks as well as advantages—they serve, for example, those elementary-school cubes of ice cream that come in silver foil. Have a grilled cheese and a Coke and watch as people from all walks of life try to sober up before they head home.

At **Afterwords,** the restaurant adjoining Kramerbooks near Dupont Circle, the desserts are many and the lattes are generous, and really, what more can you ask in the wee hours? If your companions are invariably late, it's the ideal choice, since patrons can browse in the Kramerbooks fiction section instead of sitting glumly at a table for one. Although Afterwords does close at 1am on school nights, it's open 'round the clock on weekends. There's often a line late at night (hey, not much else is open, remember?), but fortunately the waiting area abuts the store's self-help section.

The Ethiope dope... Washington reportedly has more Ethiopian restaurants than anywhere else in the country, seemingly all of which are in Adams-Morgan. Ethiopian cuisine is nothing if not fun to eat: All the orders come together on a large platter and are eaten with the hands using *injera,* a spongy tortilla-like bread. At **Meskarem,** diners have the option of eating from the country's traditional low-to-the-ground basket-tables. Soft, indigenous music plays in the background; the food can be terrifically spicy, but the ambience is mild. Some locals favor no-frills **Red Sea** across the street, with its oilcloth-covered tables and faded travel posters. The menu here includes enough meatless side dishes for vegetarians to eat well, and features such non-Ethiopian desserts as chocolate cake. Decor aside, there's not much difference between these two spots: Both menus feature the same dishes, which taste delicious at both restaurants.

Tex-Mex... Everybody seems to love the Georgetown **Austin Grill,** despite its idiotic layout (whose idea was it to have the bar blocking the way to the dining area?). Maybe it's the cowboy boots and lizards stenciled on the wall; maybe it's the daily pie specials; maybe it's the signed testimonials from Austin musicians like Michelle Shocked. Stop thinking about it and order a Swirlie, a combination lime-and-strawberry margarita. The food is your standard burrito/fajita/enchilada, but the daily pie specials are amazing—the banana pie is not to be passed up. Further up Wisconsin Avenue, campy **Cactus Cantina** serves the city's best Tex-Mex fare—and, more importantly, *sopaipillas,* puffy, deep-fried Mexican pastries dribbled with cinnamon and honey. Sort of like kudzu vines, this place has a tendency to take over adjoining buildings; it's hard to miss the two-story Christmas-light-wrapped cacti outside.

Calling **Red Sage** Tex-Mex is kind of like calling Buckingham Palace a crash pad. The most talked-about restaurant in Washington, Red Sage has been so trendy so long (practically as long as Bill Clinton has been in office), it's now trendy to not like it; it was dissed by Joe Klein in *Primary Colors* for its "haute, high-concept, hyperdesigned, if not quite distinguished, Tex-Mex cuisine." Be that as it may, the multimillion-dollar decorating job alone is worth a trip—it's a sprawling underground cavern hung with antler light fixtures and the like—and the food not only tastes outstanding, it is presented like a work of art. Order potatoes and squash and you don't get a lump of potatoes and a lump of squash, you get a vertical column of potatoes enclosed in a wrapping of squash strips and drizzled with cheese in a contrasting color. The one catch is that Red Sage isn't really open all that late—it shoos diners out the door at 10:30 most nights—but the upstairs chili bar, which also has the merit of being less expensive, stays open an hour later on weeknights, two hours later on weekends.

Southern accents... These days, Southern food doesn't just mean Velveeta macaroni-and-cheese. Downtown **Georgia Brown's** has vaguely arboreal ironwork decorations on the walls and ceiling and serves damn good Southern perennials like catfish and mashed potatoes with a stylish twist. It's a favorite of Mayor Marion Barry and newsies who work down the street at the *Washington Post*. **Old Glory,** a informal Georgetown spinoff of Georgia Brown's, has reasonably authentic fare that falls somewhere between haute Southern and the real thing, and a half-dozen different barbecue sauces to boot. Old Glory celebrates Elvis Presley's birthday each year with a party and cake; if you're looking for a place to watch *Blue Hawaii* while sucking on the best ribs in town, this is it.

Also in Georgetown, the **Music City Roadhouse,** which sometimes evokes the clamorous roadhouse spirit a little too successfully, does have appropriately Southern attributes like huge portions of down-home food and a gospel brunch. Fried catfish, zingy coleslaw, greens cooked for hours so the juices swap all around—mmm-mmm. Alexandria's **King St. Blues** is the kind of place that actually has blue-plate specials. The meat loaf on Mondays is especially good, as is their signature barbecue sauce and the world's best take on onion rings—the incomparable onion tangle. The wackiness level is notched pretty high (dig the Pee Wee Herman doll on a full-size bicycle suspended from the ceiling).

The great outdoors... Though **Sequoia** is not a great restaurant, it does have a great view: right on the Georgetown waterfront, with three terraced floors overlooking the Potomac. The well-dressed Sequoia customers—from sweaty-palmed young men hoping to impress their prom dates to middle-aged professional couples—dine on nouvelle American fare. The seafood is your best bet, though some people make special trips to Sequoia just for their Bloody Marys. On breezy summer evenings it's easy to ignore the fact that the food is no great shakes (for great shakes, go to the Dupont Circle bookstore/cafe, **Afterwords**). Be sure to look down the river from Sequoia toward the Kennedy Center and see why one critic called it "that big Kleenex box on the Potomac." The rooftop deck at **Star of Siam,** one of the city's best Thai restaurants, offers a somewhat different vista: the crowded sidewalk cafes and clubs that line Adams-Morgan's 18th Street strip some three stories below. Order some spicy Thai curry or a delectable *tom kha gai* (a cilantro-heavy chicken-and-coconut-milk soup) and chill out.

Burger meisters... Clyde's in Georgetown is known for its delicious burgers—turkey as well as beef, topped with all sorts of mushrooms, onions, cheeses, etc.—and for being the place whose lunchtime special inspired the Starland Vocal Band's 1976 hit "Afternoon Delight." Sample the large draft beer selection, study the model airplanes dangling from the ceiling, and try to get the tune out of your head. If you're pre- or postclubbing it on U Street, know that corner-bar-ish **Polly's Cafe** has particularly succulent burgers that come with a variety of toppings. In fact, come here even if you're not doing the U Street circuit—the food is great, and not just the burgers.

The Latin beat... There seems to be something inherently festive about tapas. Downtown's **Jaleo** is a case in point. Located next door to the Shakespeare Theatre, this bustling restaurant probably has the best tapas in town, with more than 40 selections to choose among, and a striking floor-to-ceiling flamenco mural. The crowd is heavy on yuppies trying out their newly acquired gold cards. In Adams-Morgan, hyper-trendy **Tom Tom** hires an artist to work on a painting on the premises in order to create atmosphere (think of it as an expensive alternative to potted ferns). A little of this kind of thing goes a long way, but the tapas are worth it. Suggestions: The goat-cheese spread, the roasted elephant-garlic clove, and the potato pizza. If you've always wondered what people mean when they say a place has a "party atmosphere," check out **Coco Loco** downtown, where the sensory overload may cause you to neglect your Brazilian-Mexican food—but don't. Look out for bands of waiters milling about with skewers of flavorful Brazilian meat, or brush them off and focus on the exhaustive tapas selection. Though billed as "Mexican tapas," they don't seem particularly different form Spanish tapas, but hey, they're good, so who cares? **The Grill From Ipanema** in Adams-Morgan specializes in rich Brazilian stews, though it also serves alligator (yes, it does taste like chicken). Diners sit beneath manmade palm trees—not quite the same thing as being on a carioca-laden Rio beach, but not bad.

Totally franc... **Bistro Française** and **Au Pied du Cochon** are both in Georgetown and both known for being open when little else is. Bistro Française is more upscale, with tablecloths and a respectable classic French menu that features things like squab and coq au vin; it even offers a 10:30pm–1am *prix fixe* menu. At Au Pied du Cochon, what you sacrifice in food quality and ambience (the glass-enclosed nonsmoking section is alongside a busy bus stop) you make up for with buzz; the clientele is a mix of student types battling hangovers and couples in formal-wear on their way home. In general, Au Pied's "cuisine" is like French-themed Denny's food, but the onion soup here is to die for.

Nouvelle American... U Street's funky, high-ceilinged **Utopia** is hung with an ever-changing exhibit of local art—often good, often bad, all for sale. But even if you're aesthetically disinclined, there's a fried brie appetizer so good that disputes over the last bite have severed lifelong friendships. The crowd is young, relaxed, and hip, and on Thursdays they chair-dance to live Brazilian music. Also situated amid the hubbub of the U Street club scene, **Polly's Cafe** is sort of a hip version of the "Cheers" bar—the alternative artists on the jukebox and the racially diverse, easygoing clientele make the difference. More restaurant than bar, it features a surprisingly sophisticated menu that includes creative pastas and a superlative hot artichoke dip. **Trumpets** has two happily coexisting personae: a mostly gay clientele congregates in the pink-walled "Drama Lounge," while epicures of all kinds hit the dining room for dishes such as salmon pizza and fried okra. It's campy enough to feature "Low Fat" and "Don't Ask, Don't Tell" menu selections, yet has cuisine refined enough to win raves from the *Post*'s exacting restaurant critic. Easy to miss, Trumpets is located down a flight of stairs below a street-level dry cleaner not far from Dupont Circle.

For establishment types... The truthfully named **Old Ebbitt Grill**—it dates from 1856—is a block from the White House and has the clientele to prove it. (No, not Bill—the so-called presidential McDonalds is in the other direction.) This stodgy leather-and-sporting-print eatery is, especially since the demise of the legendary Duke Ziebart's, *the* restaurant of choice for dealmakers, power brokers, and influence peddlers. (Less so the later it gets; the concentration of politicians is probably highest at midday.) On the far side of the massive, U-shaped bar, a mountain of ice chills an excellent raw bar; the rest of the menu offers heavy expense-account fare—big steaks and the like. The food's pretty good, but the men's-club atmosphere is oppressive. A less expensive alternative for curiosity seekers is the **Ebbitt Express** next door.

For anti-establishment types... There's nowhere else in D.C. like **Food for Thought** in the Dupont Circle area, with its hat-passing folk singers, spaced-out waiters and waitresses whose true vocation is poetry, and a huge community notice board where people look for drummers and lost cats and offer to type your résumé. A lot of people, from old lefties to young Phishheads, are no doubt drawn just by the coffeehouse atmosphere. This being a town with *no* vegetarian options, Food for Thought is definitely the vegetarian's best bet (and even it has some meat dishes). Vegetarians—and vegans, for that matter—can eat well here, on satisfying fare such as the hummus or tofu sandwiches or a bowl of vegetarian chili.

On the cheap... It may take some looking, but there certainly are antidotes to D.C.'s overabundance of expensive food, and a number of them stay open good and late. **Booeymonger,** for example, offers fat sandwiches with silly names (my fave is the Patty Hearst—turkey, bacon, melted cheese, and Russian dressing on an English muffin). The decor is strictly utilitarian, but the food sure delivers value for money. You'll dine—or eat, at any rate—with students and shoppers in the daytime and, late at night, with the can't-quite-face-heading-home-yet set. There's one in Georgetown and another in Friendship Heights. Unlike most of the trendy spots along U Street, storied **Ben's Chili Bowl**—a vintage diner wedged in next to the Lincoln Theater—has been around since this area was famous as D.C.'s "Black Broadway" four decades ago. Serving up hot dog after hot dog slathered in chili, it's the ideal stop on the way home after closing down a club. Cafeteria-style **Zorba's,** steps away from the Dupont Circle Metro escalators, offers pretty good, pretty cheap Greek—try the spanikopita, pass on the baklava. Everyone on their way to or coming back from any place in Dupont Circle is likely to stop at Zorba's, making for a crowd as varied as the passengers in a Metro car.

What **Burrito Brothers** lacks in sophistication it makes up for with the sheer volume of its hearty, unembellished, fantastic burritos. You could fit a half dozen Taco Bell burritos inside one of Burrito Brothers'. The service here is mostly takeout, though there is limited—and often hotly contested—counter space for eating in. You can't get a traditional burrito at **Wrapworks,** with branches in Georgetown and Dupont Circle, but you can get overstuffed designer burritos—they call them "wraps," probably because they're so un-Mexican—filled with a wide variety of innards, such as curried chicken and grilled vegetables, to complement the overdesigned industrial decor (think late "Miami Vice"). A different species of food entirely, but not bad on its own terms. And they'll put a vitamin in your fruit smoothie if you pay a little extra.

Pizza e pasta... Before anybody ever heard of portobello mushrooms there was **Armand's Chicago Pizzeria,** a classic pizza parlor in Tenleytown with a blaring TV, red plastic cups, and gooey deep-dish pizza. They've added some California Pizza Kitchen–style innovations to the menu, but their standard spinach and garlic is still the best. For those who are extremely impulsive or just in a hurry there's an Armand's slice window down the street (it's open Sunday–Thursday until 11pm, weekends until midnight). Georgetown's **Faccia Luna** is in a basement location next door to the always crowded Austin Grill; when exasperated would-be Grillers bail out of line, they come here—and keep coming back, especially for the unrivaled ricotta pizza. Handy to U Street's late-night trendiness is **Coppi's,** a designer-pizza joint named after the Italian bicyclist and decorated with cycling paraphernalia. The tables are so close together that the steam from your neighbor's cappuccino will fog your glasses, but the young, urbane customers here are usually talking too much to eavesdrop. Equally good designer pizzas are available at Dupont Circle's ever-mobbed **Pizza Paradiso**—try the zillion-cheese pizza and anything with red onions or prosciutto. You may have to wait as long as half an hour for a table, but the scent from the brick oven and the snug but cheerful Mediterranean decor make the wait tolerable.

Of Asian persuasion... D.C. has a multitude of Asian eateries to choose from, but they tend to shutter up by 11pm. Among the exceptions: Stylish **Raku,** a favorite of Dupont Circle yuppies, which serves a range of Asian cuisines, all well executed, and has an ultramodern, exposed-pipe interior. Be sure to sample the sorbet. At **Tony Cheng's Mongolian Barbecue,** one of many Chinese spots within sight of the gaudy Chinatown arch, you pick your own raw ingredients and watch while they're grilled in front of you by theatrical chefs. The food is quite good, but the showmanship is certainly part of the draw. For stellar outdoor Thai dining, there's the **Star of Siam** in Adams-Morgan, where you can gaze at the Washington Monument as you sip rich Thai iced coffee on the spacious roof deck. The food is affordable, the view priceless. Cleveland Park's **Yenching Palace,** with its early-1960s facade and signage, is an unofficial local landmark: It was here that emissaries of Khrushchev and Kennedy brought the Cuban Missile Crisis to a halt in 1962, perhaps over the steamed dumplings. The Yenching does a brisk take-out business; the entrées tend to have that eaten-from-a-carton feel even when consumed on site.

Just desserts... You might want to plan your trip around **Ben & Jerry's** nationwide Free Cone Day in the spring, especially if your local IGA doesn't stock the Vermont duo's ever-farther-out new flavors, like Coffee, Coffee, Buzz, Buzz, Buzz. The Adams-Morgan and Georgetown locations both stay open good and late. The homemade ice cream at **Thomas Sweet,** which stands on a busy Georgetown street corner, comes in a Baskin-Robbins-like spectrum of flavors, but this low-key parlor is blessedly free of pink decorating accents. Seating is limited and the line can snake out the door on summer nights. Finally, there's the aforementioned **Afterwords,** the cafe adjoining Kramerbooks, which features the colossal "Dysfunctional Family Sundae." Say no more.

Late Night Dining: Index

$$$ more than $30
$$ $10–$20
$ Less than $10
Prices are per person, not including drinks and tip.

***Note:** Where no Metro stop is listed, a restaurant is best reached by taxi or car. The nearest Metro station to Georgetown is Foggy Bottom–GWU, a 15-minute walk or short cab ride away.*

2 Quail. Where Laura Ashley meets haute cuisine.... *Tel 202/543–8030. 320 Massachusetts Ave., NE. Open Mon–Thur to 10:30pm, Fri–Sat to 11:15pm, Sun to 10pm. Union Station Metro. $$$* **(see p. 147)**

Afterwords. Combination restaurant and bookstore, home of the well-worth-it $5 milkshake.... *Tel 202/387–1462. 1517 Connecticut Ave., NW. Open Sun–Thur to 1am, Fri–Sat 24 hours. Dupont Circle Metro. $$* **(see pp. 148, 150, 155)**

Armand's Chicago Pizzeria. The city's best old-fashioned pizza—i.e., pepperoni and mushroom as opposed to artichoke and goat cheese. Bargain freaks will eat themselves sick at the daily pizza and salad buffet.... *Tel 202/363–6268. 4231 Wisconsin Ave., NW. Open Sun–Thur to 11pm, Fri–Sat to 1am. Tenleytown–AU Metro. $–$$* **(see p. 154)**

Au Pied du Cochon. Left-Bankish French bistro in Georgetown, always open.... *Tel 202/333–5440. 1335 Wisconsin Ave., NW. Open 24 hours. $$* **(see pp. 147, 151)**

Austin Grill. Affable upper Georgetown Tex-Mex, very popular (there are spinoffs in Bethesda and Alexandria, too).... *Tel 202/337–8080. 2404 Wisconsin Ave., NW. Open Sun–Mon to 10:30pm, Tue–Thur to 11pm, Fri–Sat to midnight. $$* **(see p. 148)**

Ben & Jerry's. Heath Bar Crunch. Accept no substitutes.... *Tel 202/667–6677, 2503 Champlain St., NW, open daily to 11pm, Woodley Park-Zoo Metro; tel 202/965–2222, 3135 M St., NW, open Sun–Wed to 11pm, Fri–Sat to 1am; tel 202/842–5882, 1100 Pennsylvania Ave., NW, open daily to 9pm, McPherson Square Metro. $* **(see p. 155)**

Ben's Chili Bowl. Justly famed for, that's right, chili. Get it in a bowl or piled onto a burger or hot dog.... *Tel 202/667–0909. 1213 U St., NW. Open Mon–Thur to 2am, Fri–Sat to 4am, Sun to 8pm. U Street-Cardozo Metro. $* **(see p. 153)**

Bistro Française. Moderately upscale French bistro in Georgetown.... *Tel 202/338–3830. 3128 M St., NW. Open Sun–Thur to 3am, Fri–Sat to 4am. $$* **(see pp. 147, 151)**

Booeymonger. The place to go for big, drippy sandwiches. Sample the cinnamon coffee.... *Tel 202/333–4810, 3265 Prospect St., NW, open daily to midnight; tel 202/686–5805, 5252 Wisconsin Ave., NW, open Sun–Thur to 1am, Fri–Sat to 2am, Friendship Heights Metro. $* **(see p. 153)**

Burrito Brothers. Big fat burritos that are heavy enough to knock someone down with.... *Tel 202/265–4048, 2418 18th St., NW, Woodley Park-Zoo Metro; tel 202/332–2308, 1524 Connecticut Ave., NW, Dupont Circle Metro; tel 202/965–3963, 3273 M St., NW. Open Sun–Wed to midnight, Thur–Sat to 3am. $* **(see p. 153)**

Cactus Cantina. Ever-expanding local favorite serves generous portions of hearty Tex-Mex fare.... *Tel 202686-722. 3300 Wisconsin Ave., NW. Open Sun–Thur to 11pm, Fri–Sat to midnight. Tenleytown–AU Metro. $$* **(see p. 149)**

Cities. Trendy Adams-Morgan nightspot features the food and decor of a different city every few years. Now playing: Istanbul.... *Tel 202/328–7194. 2424 18th St., NW. Open*

Mon–Thur to 11pm, Fri–Sat to 11:30pm. Woodley Park–Zoo Metro. $$–$$$ **(see p. 146)**

Clyde's. Classic American fare—from bacon cheeseburgers on up—dominates the menu at this Georgetown mainstay.... *Tel 202/333–9180. 3236 M St., NW. Open Mon–Thur to 10:30pm, Fri–Sat to 11:30pm, Sun to 10pm. $$* **(see p. 150)**

Coco Loco. Colorful Brazilian-Mexican restaurant and nightclub features everything from tapas to the merengue.... *Tel 202/289–2626. 810 7th St., NW. Restaurant open Mon–Thur to 10pm, Fri–Sat to 11pm. Gallery Place–Chinatown Metro. $$* **(see p. 151)**

Coppi's. The seating is elbow-to-elbow at this hip designer-pizza joint on U Street.... *Tel 202/319–7773. 1414 U St., NW. Open Mon–Thur to midnight, Fri–Sat to 1am, Sun to 11pm. U Street–Cardozo Metro. $$* **(see p. 154)**

Ebbitt Express. See ***Old Ebbitt Grill***

Faccia Luna. Casual Italian eatery in upper Georgetown.... *Tel 202/337–3132. 2400 Wisconsin Ave., NW. Open Sun–Thur to 11pm, Fri–Sat to midnight. $$* **(see p. 154)**

Food for Thought. Washington's foremost—okay, only—bohemian hangout. You won't find vegan brownies anywhere else in the city.... *Tel 202/797–1095. 1738 Connecticut Ave., NW. Open Sun–Thur to 12:30am, Fri–Sat to 2am. Dupont Circle Metro. $–$$* **(see p. 152)**

Georgetown Cafe. As a restaurant, its chief attribute is its hours of operation.... *Tel 202/333–0215. 1623 Wisconsin Ave., NW. Open 24 hours. $* **(see p. 147)**

Georgia Brown's. Bastion of nouvelle Southern cuisine—the only upscale restaurant around where you can get stuff like lima beans and grits.... *Tel 202/393–4499. 1500 K St., NW. Open Sun–Thur to 11pm, Fri–Sat to midnight. Farragut North Metro. $$* **(see p. 149)**

The Grill From Ipanema. A vegetarian's nightmare, this Brazilian restaurant has the meatiest menu in the city, and the funniest name.... *Tel 202/986–0757. 1858 Columbia*

Rd., NW. Open Mon–Thur to 11pm, Fri–Sat to midnight, Sun to 10pm. Woodley Park-Zoo Metro. $$ **(see p. 151)**

Hard Rock Cafe. You've seen it all before: Pete Townshend's guitar, mediocre burgers and fries, tourists in a T-shirt-buying frenzy.... *Tel 202/737–7625. 999 E St., NW. Open Sun–Thur to midnight, Fri–Sat to 1am. Metro Center. $$***(see pp. 146)**

Jaleo. One word: Tapas.... *Tel 202/628–7949. 480 7th St., NW. Open Sun–Mon to 10pm, Tue–Thur to 11:30pm, Fri–Sat to midnight. Archives–Navy Memorial Metro. $$* **(see p. 151)**

King St. Blues. Determinedly wacky Southern eatery in Old Town.... *Tel 703/836–8800. 112 St. Asaph St., Alexandria, VA. Open Sun–Thur to 10pm, Fri–Sat to midnight. King Street Metro. $$* **(see p. 150)**

Meskarem. Eat Ethiopian food from ethnographically correct knee-level basket tables.... *Tel 202/462–4100. 2434 18th St., NW. Open Sun–Thur to midnight, Fri–Sat to 1am. Woodley Park–Zoo Metro. $$* **(see p. 148)**

Music City Roadhouse Insomniac Georgetown neighbors put a stop to the live music, but this place still has something of a roadhouse flavor—any place that displays Tanya Tucker's old jeans.... *Tel 202/337–4444. 1050 30th St., NW. Open Sun–Thur to midnight, Fri–Sat to 2am. $$* **(see p. 150)**

Old Ebbitt Grill. Haunted by both actual politicians and people hoping to see actual politicians. The downscale Ebbitt Express is next door.... *Tel 202/347–4800. 675 15th St., NW. Open Mon–Thur to 1am, Fri to 2am, Sat to 1am, Sun to midnight. McPherson Square Metro. $$* **(see p. 152)**

Old Glory. What better monument to Elvis than a barbecue joint?... *Tel 202/337–3406. 3139 M St., NW. Open Sun–Thur to 1am, Fri–Sat to 2am. $–$$* **(see p. 149)**

Pizza Paradisio. Mussel pizza anyone? The perpetually crowded source of Dupont Circle's favorite pizza.... *Tel 202/223–1245. 2029 P St., NW. Open Mon–Thur to 11pm, Fri–Sat to midnight, Sun to 10pm. Dupont Circle Metro. $$*

(see p. 154)

Planet Hollywood. Self-described "restaurant and entertainment complex"—the on-site retail outlet is often more crowded than the dining room.... *Tel 202/783–7827. 1101 Pennsylvania Ave., NW. Open daily to 1am. Metro Center. $$* **(see p. 146)**

Polly's Cafe. Comfy U Street restaurant and bar with lots of exposed brick and devoted regulars.... *Tel 202/265–8385. 1342 U St., NW. Open Sun–Thur to midnight, Fri–Sat to 2am. U Street–Cardozo Metro. $$* **(see pp. 151, 152)**

Raku. Sample the cuisine of several countries at once at this fashionable pan-Asian eatery.... *Tel 202/265–7258. 1900 Q St., NW. Open Mon–Thur to midnight, Fri–Sat to 2am, Sun to 10pm. Dupont Circle Metro. $$* **(see p. 154)**

Red Sage. If you're only going to eat out once in D.C., this admittedly over-the-top Southwestern restaurant is the place to do it.... *Tel 202/638–4444. 605 14th St., NW. Restaurant open Mon–Sat to 10:30pm, Sun to 10pm; chili bar open Sun–Thur to 11:30pm, Fri–Sat to 12:30am. Metro Center. $$$* **(see pp. 147, 149)**

Red Sea. No-frills Ethiopian in Adams-Morgan.... *Tel 202/483–5000. 2463 18th St., NW. Open Sun–Thur to 11pm, Fri–Sat to midnight. Woodley Park–Zoo Metro. $$* **(see p. 149)**

Sequoia. Food with a view.... *Tel 202/944–4200. 3000 K St., NW. Open Sun–Thur to 1am, Fri–Sat to 2:30am. $$* **(see p. 150)**

Star of Siam. A near-perfect scenario: Thai food on an Adams-Morgan rooftop in summer.... *Tel 202/986–4133. 2446 18th St., NW. Open Sun–Thur to 11pm, Fri–Sat to midnight. Woodley Park–Zoo Metro. $$* **(see pp. 150, 155)**

Tastee Diner. The perpetual neon sign in the window says it all: OPEN. EATS.... *Tel 301/652–3970. 7731 Woodmont Ave., Bethesda, MD, Bethesda Metro; tel 301/589–8171, 8516 Georgia Ave., Silver Spring, MD, Silver Spring Metro. Open 24 hours. $* **(see p. 148)**

Thomas Sweet. Ice cream, frozen yogurt, and the like, made on the premises. And no one proselytizing about saving the earth.... *Tel 202/337–0616. 3214 P St., NW. Open Sun–Thur to 11pm, Fri–Sat to midnight. $* **(see p. 155)**

Tom Tom. Superb tapas, but the pretension can be stultifying. You make the call.... *Tel 202/588–1300. 2335 18th St., NW. Open Mon–Thur to 11pm, Fri–Sun to midnight. Woodley Park–Zoo Metro. $$* **(see p. 151)**

Tony Cheng's Mongolian Barbecue. Pick your own ingredients and hand them to a chef, or cook your own raw ingredients at the table in a pot of hot broth.... *Tel 202/842–8669. 619 H St., NW. Open Mon–Thur to 11pm, Fri–Sat to midnight, Sun to 10pm. Gallery Place–Chinatown Metro. $$* **(see p. 154)**

Trumpets. Top-notch restaurant that is also a gay nightclub.... *Tel 202/232–4141. 1633 Q St., NW. Restaurant open daily to 11pm. Dupont Circle Metro. $$* **(see p. 152)**

Utopia. This hip art-space eatery has an eclectic menu and keeps late hours.... *Tel 202/483-7669. 1418 U St., NW. Open Mon–Fri to 2am, Sat to 3am, Sun to 1:30am. U Street-Cardozo Metro. $$* **(see p. 152)**

Wrapworks. Overstuffed variations on the lowly burrito.... *Tel 202/265–4200, Q St. at Connecticut Ave., NW, Dupont Circle Metro; tel 202/333–0220, 1079 Wisconsin Ave., NW. Open Sun–Thur to 11pm, Fri–Sat to midnight. $* **(see p. 153)**

Xing Kuba. Modish Cuban-Asian cuisine and a name that dares you to try and pronounce it.... *Tel 202/965–0665. 2218 Wisconsin Ave., NW. Open Sun–Thur to 10:15pm, Fri–Sat to 11:15pm. $$–$$$* **(see p. 146)**

Yenching Palace. The steamed dumplings are good, but the historical associations are better.... *Tel 202/362–8200. 3524 Connecticut Ave., NW. Open Sun–Thur to 11pm, Fri–Sat to 11:30pm. Cleveland Park Metro. $–$$* **(see p. 155)**

Zorba's. Self-service Greek food for cheap.... *Tel 202/387–8555. 1612 20th St., NW. Open Mon–Wed to 11:30pm, Thur–Sat to 2:30am, Sun to 10:30pm. Dupont Circle Metro. $* **(see p. 153)**

down and dirty

All-night groceries... There aren't any full-fledged supermarkets in the district open 24 hours (although there's a proliferation of designer convenience stores in Dupont Circle and Georgetown whose prices can make actual supermarkets worth looking for). The **Giant** at 3336 Wisconsin Ave., NW (tel 202/244–5922) is usually open around the clock, however, closing only from 11pm Saturday night to 7am Sunday morning, and from 10pm Sunday night to 7am Monday. The **Safeway** at 1855 Wisconsin Ave., NW (tel 202/333–3223) stays open until 11pm Monday through Saturday, 10pm Sunday. The latter is known locally as "the social Safeway," but don't bother looking for love by the canned yams—its reputed singles scene is a product of wishful thinking.

All-night pharmacies... The **CVS** drugstores on Dupont Circle (tel 202/833–5704) and Thomas Circle (tel 202/628–0720) are open 24 hours. The Thomas Circle location lies in an area rife with hookers—the neighborhood's distinctive parking regulations (on most nearby streets, "stopping" is forbidden between 9pm and 5am) testify to the District government's ineffective efforts to curb prostitution there.

Babysitters... Most hotel concierges keep a list of local babysitters on hand. Other options include **Wee Sit** (tel 703/764–1542); **Babysitters Inc.** (tel 202/234–5900); **Chevy Chase Baby Sitters** (tel 301/916–2694); and **Mother's Aides Inc.** (tel 703/250–0700).

Buses... The fare for D.C. **Metrobuses** is $1.10, which must be in exact change. Buses run from 6am to 11:30pm daily, and rarely arrive as scheduled. Learning the D.C. bus system is probably a fruitless undertaking for a short-term visitor, but call **Metrobus** (tel 202/637–7000) and you may be able to get explicit instructions on how to get from where you are to where you need to go by bus. Schedules are available on the buses themselves, or at the main office at the Metro Center station. Bus transfers are available at Metro stations so that trips may be continued by bus without paying an additional fare.

Car rentals... If you absolutely must drive in the District, rental cars are available from **Avis** (tel 800/831–2847); **Budget** (tel 800/527–0700); **Dollar** (tel 800/800–4000); **Enterprise** (tel 800/325–8007); **Hertz** (tel 800/654–3131); and **Thrifty** (tel 800/367–2277), among others. Want to impress the valet-parking attendant? Try **Beverly Hills**

Rentals (tel 703/749–5372), which will put you in a Mercedes, Lexus, or BMW. Heard about D.C.'s potholes? **Cenit** (tel 202/882–8817) specializes in pickups and 4-wheel-drive vehicles.

Driving... Navigating by car in Washington presents some significant challenges. It's important to remember, while white-knuckled behind the wheel, that Pierre L'Enfant designed the city in 1791, when horse-drawn vehicles were the primary mode of transportation. The city is divided into four quadrants: Northwest, Northeast, Southwest, and Southeast. When heading for a specific address, be sure to note the quadrant designation—NW, NE, SW, or SE—to avoid ending up at 108 Q Street, NW instead of 108 Q Street, NE. (In addition to wasting time, getting it wrong can be a major safety blunder.) The city's numbered streets run north-south, with numbers increasing as you move east or west from Capitol Hill. Lettered streets run east-west, climbing the alphabet as you move north or south from the Mall. The avenues, named for states, run diagonally, intersecting with the east-west and north-south streets at traffic circles. (Repeat after me: Cars already in traffic circles have the right of way.) This sounds more straightforward than it is. Consider, for instance, that there's no J Street, or that California alone among the states was designated a horizontal street instead of a diagonal avenue. Several major thoroughfares become one-way during rush hour (7–9:30am and 4–6:30pm) or have lanes that change direction during rush hour to accommodate heavy inbound or outbound traffic, so watch the signs like a hawk. On top of all this, special events such as marches and demonstrations can create traffic Armageddon. Watch out for cars with red, white, and blue diplomatic plates—"dips" have a well-deserved reputation for maniacal driving. Lastly, there is a notable dearth of gas stations in the district. Make a note of the one nearest you, and don't get low on gas under the assumption that there's a pump on every corner—t'ain't so.

Chauffeurs... If you liked the look of the presidential motorcade and want to hire your own, try **Classic Limousines Inc.** (tel 202/338–2632); **Reston Limousine** (tel 202/797–0500); **Bethany Limousine Service** (tel 202/857–0440); or **Capital City Limousines** (tel 202/484–0200).

Emergencies... Dial **911,** as always. The **police** nonemergency number is 202/727–1010. **Georgetown University Medical Center** (tel 202/687–2000, 3800 Reservoir Rd., NW) and **George Washington University Medical Center** (tel 202/994–1000, 901 23rd St., NW) are the city's two largest hospitals, both with 24-hour emergency rooms. For lesser emergencies, the **Interactive Donnelley Talking Yellow Pages** (tel 301/816–1616) offers an extensive touch-tone menu providing information on everything from Bunions (2880) to Documents Required to File for Bankruptcy (1117). An overlong stay in the district may require knowledge of both topics.

Festivals and special events...

January: If you're into long-range planning, January 20—**Presidential Inauguration Day**—is pretty exciting every four years. Traffic becomes limo gridlock and public transportation is packed with people in formalwear. A cool $150 will get you a ticket to an inaugural ball, where they don't serve food, it's too crowded to dance, and the tall guy in front of you blocks your view of the president.

March: The annual **Cherry Blossom Festival** celebrates the blooming of the Tidal Basin's 300,000 cherry trees, a gift from Japan in 1912, between late March and mid-April. The pale-pink profusion, which can enchant even flower haters, generally lasts 7 to 12 days, barring bad weather. While the festival's main event is a daytime parade, many people drive by or walk beneath the blossoms at night to avoid the annual cherry-blossom traffic jam. For more info call the National Park Service (tel 202/619–7222) or check out the NPS's cherry-blossom website (http://www.nps.gov/nacc/cherry).

April: **Filmfest DC** (tel 202/274–6810), Washington's international film festival, takes place in cinemas around town from April 23 to May 4 (see The Arts). Filmfest DC's fare can be uneven, but there's always a gem or two among its offerings.

June: Washington's annual **Gay Pride Day** celebration (tel 202/298–0970), which seems to grow exponentially each year, includes events of all shapes and sizes as well as the daytime opening parade to the festival site. Shakespeare Theatre's annual **Free for All** (tel 202/547–3230) presents a Shakespeare play in a 2-week run outdoors at Carter Barron Amphitheater (see "The Arts"); tickets are available on a first-come, first-served basis. **Wolf Trap** music park (tel 703/218–6500) holds two annual music festivals this month at its Filene Center: The **Louisiana Swamp Romp** and the **Jazz and Blues Festival**, both running for several days. See The Arts for more on Wolf Trap's summer activities.

July: Every summer, the **Festival of American Folklife** (tel 202/357–2700) pitches its tents on the National Mall. This tribute to folk culture—its events include regional cooking demonstrations and performances of indigenous music—spotlights two parts of the country every year. Plenty of folks (if not culture) invade the Mall on **Independence Day,** where the nation's annual July 4th hoopla is capped by a fireworks display at 9pm on the Washington Monument grounds. The volume of people who turn out on the Fourth is so high (about a half million each year) that Metro turnstiles are locked open and Metro officials stand at the exits collecting farecards in industrial-size trash bins. For info call the National Park Service at 202/619–7222. Through July and August, the Source Theatre Company's monthlong **Washington Theatre Festival** (Tel 202/462–1073) presents 70 new plays, workshops, readings, and the 10-Minute Play Competition—an especially popular event in the city that elevated the sound bite to an art form.

September: **Adams-Morgan Day** (tel 202/332–3292) is an annual celebration of the funky D.C. neighborhood known for its ethnic restaurants and scarcity of parking places. The festival's notorious rowdiness has resulted in the gradual curtailing of its evening events, which once lasted far into the night but now shut down around 7 pm.

October: Halloween in Washington is synonymous with the annual **high-heel race** (for men) down 17th Street, NW. This high-camp event is sponsored by the Whitman-Walker Clinic (tel 202/797–3500).

December: The lighting of the stories-high **national Christmas tree** in front of the Capitol building isn't much of an event in itself, but the tree is a fine destination for nighttime drives thereafter. Call the National Park Service (tel 202/619–7222) to confirm the date of the lighting.

Free stuff... One positive aspect of its being a federal city is that Washington has an unusually large number of free events and activities. This is particularly true during the summer months when, for instance, military bands give outdoor concerts most nights of the week at the Sylvan Theater near the Washington Monument and on the Capitol's East Terrace (see The Arts). Call the National Park Service (tel 202/619–7222) or check local newspapers for listings.

Gay and lesbian resources... The ***Washington Blade,*** D.C.'s increasingly formidable weekly gay newspaper, is distributed on Fridays; it's available free from local retailers and bookstores. The paper's listings offer an exhaustive compendium of gay-friendly services and gay-oriented entertainment events. Other community resources include the **Gay and Lesbian Switchboard** (tel 202/628–4667) and the 24-hour **Gay and Lesbian Hot Line** (tel 202/833–3234).

Hotlines... Post-Haste (tel 202/334–9000) is a *Washington Post* telephone service for information on weather, spectator sports, golf, fishing, restaurants, lottery results, and much more. **Kennedy Center Performance Information** (tel 202/467–4600, 800/444–1324) gives details on upcoming performances at the center and lets you charge tickets. Various local radio stations operate their own hot lines as well: the **WWDC Concert and Information Line** (tel 301/587–0300) lists mainstream and alternative rock music attractions, and the **WDCU "Jazz 90" Info Line** (tel 202/274–6490) features jazz listings.

Newspapers... The ***Washington Post,*** of course, is the city's major daily. Not surprisingly, political coverage is the paper's long suit. The Weekend section, which contains mainstream movie and event listings, is published every Friday. The ***Washington Times,*** a right-wing daily owned by Sun Myung Moon's Unification Church, has an eighth of the Post's circulation. ***Washington City Paper,*** the city's alternative weekly, is distributed on Thursdays; it's available in gray street boxes at every Metro station and at retail establishments all over town. *City Paper*'s events listings—especially those for concerts, live music at clubs, readings, and offbeat events that can't afford to advertise—are by far the most comprehensive in town. All three papers are available online: the *Post* at http://www.washingtonpost.com; the *Times* at http://www.washtimes.com; and *City Paper* at http://www.washingtoncitypaper.com.

Online info... Entertainment schedules for many of D.C.'s major venues are available online: The **Kennedy Center**

(http://kennedy-center.org); **Wolf Trap** (http://www.wolf-trap.org); the **9:30 Club** (http://www.930.com); the Smithsonian Institution (http://www.si.edu); and the National Zoo (http://www.si.edu/organiza/museums/zoo/homepage/nzhome.htm). If you've really, really enjoyed your stay, the **New Homes Guide** is at http://www.homefair.com/nhg.

Parking... In Washington, no parking violation goes unpunished. The D.C. system's so efficient, officials from other countries come here to see how it's done, so take heed. Red signs with arrows and green signs with arrows indicate where and when parking is and is not legal. Read them. If you don't, you might want to pick up a copy of the book *How to Beat a D.C. Parking Ticket,* available all over the city. Be especially alert during evening rush hours, when much of the city's street parking—especially downtown and on main roadways—is illegal. In commercial areas, most on-street parking is metered, so hoard your quarters. In residential neighborhoods, cars with resident decals are allowed to park for longer periods that outsiders' cars. Many downtown and Georgetown restaurants offer valet parking, which is generally complimentary. There are well-marked commercial parking garages and parking lots in most prime tourist areas; exceptions are the U Street area and Adams-Morgan, where street parking is usually the only option. Garage parking will run you between $6 and $10, the daily maximum for a couple of hours or more.

Pet sitters... If you're traveling with a four-legged little darling and you want a night out, try ringing **Sit-a-Pet** (tel 202/362–8900) or **Pet Cetera** (tel 202/364-4941).

Phone facts... Directory assistance is **411**. Don't forget that you must dial the **301 area code** for numbers in Maryland and the **703 area code** for numbers in Virginia. These are not charged as long-distance calls. Other frequently dialed area codes are **410** for Baltimore and thereabouts, and **804** for southern Virginia; both of these are long-distance.

Radio... Local AM stations include: **WTEM** (570) for sports; **WJFK** (1300) for jazz; **WTOP** (1500) for news; **WPGC** (1580) for hip-hop; and **WWDC** (1260) for big-band. On FM, there's **WAMU** (88.5) for NPR; **WKYS** (93.9) for urban contemporary; **WHFS** (99.1) for alternative rock; **WMZQ** (98.7) for country; **WBIG**

(100.3) for oldies; **WWDC** (101.1) for hard rock; and **WGMS** (103.5) for classical.

Safety... D.C. is no longer the murder capital of America, but caution is still in order when carousing after dark. There are safe and unsafe areas in every quadrant of the District, often in close proximity to one another. In general, it's best to avoid Southeast, Northeast, and Northwest east of 14th Street after dark, unless you're with someone who knows the city. Georgetown is very safe at night, but in the U Street nightlife area and Adams-Morgan it's wise to stay alert once you've left the main thoroughfares. The Metro is wonderfully safe to ride at night; the city was recently shocked by a metro robbery, because such things are unheard of.

Subway... D.C.'s **Metrorail** (tel 202/637–7000 for information) is safe, clean, and idiot-proof. To enter the system, you need to buy a magnetic farecard, which you can do at either machines or manned booths in each station. Fares—varying from $1.10 to $3.25, based on the distance traveled and the time of day—are automatically calculated when you run your card through the turnstile on entering and leaving the system. Virtually the only drawback to the system is that it closes at midnight, bringing the nighttime activities of the young and the carless to an abrupt halt. The Metro runs 5:30am–midnight Monday–Friday, and 8am–midnight Saturday and Sunday. The one exception to this rule is on Independence Day, when the subway patriotically stays open until 2am. Easy-to-read signage at each station makes it virtually impossible to catch the wrong train. Trains are supposed to come every 10 minutes, and they actually do. No smoking or food is allowed, and you need a permit to take a bike on board. Thrill seekers should note that the Wheaton Metro station boasts the world's longest and most vertiginous escalator. A word to the wise: The most common mistake of first-time riders is to discard their farecards after they enter through the turnstile. Don't—you'll need your card in order to exit the station at your destination.

Taxis... Cabs in D.C. aren't metered like they are everywhere else (although they will be converting to a meter system in the foreseeable future). Instead, they use a byzantine zone system that charges passengers by the number of zones they pass through on a given trip. There are eight zones and innumerable subzones in the city. By law, a zone map must be posted in every cab, but they're pretty much useless for the baffled layman. One way to avoid being cheated without actually having to understand the zone system is to get a price quote over the phone in advance for the trip you plan to take. Beware hidden costs: There are surcharges for rush-hour trips, for additional passengers, and for having a cab dispatched, and expect huge price hikes for trips outside the District. Share your complaints with the **D.C. Taxi Commission** (tel 202/767–8319). **Taxi 24-hour Services** (tel 202/398–0500) dispatches cabs from 13 different cab companies. Other cab companies include **Diamond Cab** (tel 202/387–6200); **Yellow Cab** (tel 202/544–1212); and **Red Top Cab** (tel 202/328–3333). For the socially conscious, **Clean Air Cabs** (tel 202/667–7000) run on natural gas. For the extremely socially conscious, the "pedicabs" of **Potomac Pedicabs** (tel 202/744–3742 or 202/332–1732) run on human sweatpower.

Tickets... For most performing arts events, it's cheaper to buy tickets without going through an intermediary, so buy directly from the venue when possible. Policies vary; some places handle their own charge-by-phone ticketing, and don't tack on an additional charge, while others require that you come to the box office in advance and buy tickets with cash. If you don't mind coughing up the surcharge, you can reserve tickets by phone through Protix (tel 703/638–1908), which serves the 9:30 Club, Wolf Trap, and the Merriweather Post Pavilion, and through TicketMaster (tel 703/432–SEAT, 800/551–7328), which serves the Black Cat, the Capitol Ballroom, the Bayou, USAir Arena, the Birchmere, Nissan Pavilion at Stone Ridge, and the Patriot Center. TicketMaster also handles tickets to sporting events. Tickets to **Kennedy Center** events can be charged by calling 202/467–4600. **TICKETplace** (202/842–5387) offers half-price day-of-show tickets for a variety of events.

Television... In the District, the NBC affiliate is channel 4 (WRC); ABC is channel 7 (WJLA); CBS is channel 9 (WUSA); PBS is channel 26 (WETA); and Fox is channel 5 (WTTG).

Time... Synchronizing your watches? Call 202/844–1212.

Travelers with disabilities... The District's major monuments and museums are high-visibility federal property, where compliance with the Americans With Disabilities Act is a point of pride; sights such as the White House and the Washington Monument, for instance, are wheelchair accessible. (Sometimes these efforts backfire, though, as with recent complaints that the Braille at the new F.D.R. Memorial is so big that it's unreadable.) The Smithsonian Institution distributes a free brochure detailing the accessibility of all its museums as well as the National Zoo. Most city blocks have curb cuts. Public transportation is very accessible—some, though not all, city Metrobuses can accommodate wheelchairs (call Metrobus at 202/637–7000 for schedule information); all Metro stops feature elevators for disabled passengers, and Metro cars have seating for the handicapped and open space for wheelchairs. Restaurants and nightspots, however, are a mixed bag; it's best to call ahead.

Visitor information... The **Washington Convention and Visitors' Association** (tel 202/789–7000, with live operators 9am–5pm Monday—Friday, an automated information line other times) offers a wide array of touristy basics, while the **National Park Service** (tel 202/619–7222, 7:45am–4:15 pm Monday–Friday) is the best source for information about marches, demonstrations, and events on federal property, such as the Independence Day festivities on the Mall.

Weather... Tel 202/936–1212. Or just look out the window.